— PRAISE FOR —

CONSIDERING SPARROWS

"For all of my life, I've been fascinated by birds. For most of my life, I've been fascinated by theology. What could be better than a book that combines them both? In *Considering Sparrows,* Kevin Burrell draws powerful lessons about the Creator from the marvels of his creation. I have long been an avid reader of Burrell's articles and am thrilled I now have a book to read, enjoy, and recommend to others."

—TIM CHALLIES, pastor, speaker, and author of *Seasons of Sorrow*

"I love the way Burrell meticulously weaves together captivating bird stories with scripture and real-life situations, which all point to Jesus. I couldn't put this book down!"

—JILL ROMAN LORD, award-winning author of *One Night in Bethlehem* and over thirty Christian children's books

"*Considering Sparrows* takes us from swifts to starlings, crows to cranes, bowerbirds to bulbuls, as Kevin Burrell leads us further into the wondrous world we inhabit, helping us fall more deeply in love with the God who spun it all into being. Generous in its pastoral spirit, this insightful, funny, pithy work will have birders and non-birders alike singing its praises. As a birder, I couldn't put it down. As a pastor, I can't wait to share it with my church."

—COURTNEY ELLIS, author of *Looking Up: A Birder's Guide to Hope Through Grief* and host of *The Thing with Feathers* podcast

"*Considering Sparrows* is one of the most unusual books I've ever read. Not only that, it's fun and informative. I don't know a whole lot about birds, but given that I'm a longtime pastor, I know a lot about Jesus. Now, when I encounter birds, I'll think about Jesus and, sometimes, when I think about Jesus, I'll think about birds. Both will remind me that I'm loved, forgiven, and accepted by the God who created both the birds and me. Read this book and give it to your friends. They will 'rise up and call you blessed.'"

—STEVE BROWN, seminary pastor, broadcaster, author, and founder of Key Life Network, Inc.

"My life and career revolve around speed, which is why I'm grateful for a book that calls me to slow down and notice God's handiwork in the world around me. As my pastor, Kevin Burrell has long been a voice in my life pointing me to Jesus, and through this book, he continues that with grace, warmth, and wisdom."

—DAVE ALPERN, president of Joe Gibbs Racing

"I love birds! Watching them is so refreshing. So when Kevin Burrell takes me by the hand and shows me spiritual lessons from the world of birds in the letter to the Philippians, the benefits soar to the skies. I commend this book to you. You will never look at these feathered creatures the same way again—nor the book of Philippians!"

—CONRAD MBEWE, pastor of Kabwata Baptist Church and founding chancellor of the African Christian University in Lusaka, Zambia

"Every page of *Considering Sparrows* displays Kevin Burrell's devotion to Christ and his love for people. He offers us a glimpse into the wonder of the natural world in light of how pondering Scripture reveals who God is. He also shows us how the natural world gives us countless opportunities to experience the comfort, hope, and joy that we all need from the Savior of the world."

—DR. RICHARD L. PRATT, JR., president of Third Millennium Ministries

CONSIDERING SPARROWS

CONSIDERING SPARROWS

What Birds Teach Us About
Who We Are, Where We're Going,
and the Joy of Following Jesus

KEVIN BURRELL

Illustrated by Aedan Peterson
Foreword by Joni Eareckson Tada

MULTNOMAH

Multnomah

An imprint of the Penguin Random House Christian Publishing Group,
a division of Penguin Random House LLC

1745 Broadway, New York, NY 10019

waterbrookmultnomah.com

penguinrandomhouse.com

Italics in Scripture quotations reflect the author's added emphasis.

Interior illustrations: losmostachos/Adobe Stock, feather (title page);
inspiring.team/Adobe Stock, additional feathers

Library of Congress Cataloging-in-Publication Data
Names: Burrell, Kevin, 1969- author
Title: Considering sparrows / Kevin Burrell.
Description: New York, NY : Multnomah, [2026] | Includes bibliographical references.
Identifiers: LCCN 2025040388 (print) | LCCN 2025040389 (ebook) |
ISBN 9798217152261 hardcover | ISBN 9798217152278 ebook
Subjects: LCSH: Bird watchers—Religious life | Bird watching—
Religious aspects—Christianity
Classification: LCC BV4596.B57 B87 2026 (print) | LCC BV4596.B57 (ebook)
LC record available at https://lccn.loc.gov/2025040388
LC ebook record available at https://lccn.loc.gov/2025040389

Printed in the United States of America

1st Printing

First Edition

The authorized representative in the EU for product safety and compliance
is Penguin Random House Ireland, Morrison Chambers, 32 Nassau Street,
Dublin D02 YH68, Ireland. https://eu-contact.penguin.ie

BOOKMAKING TEAM: Production editor: Jessica Choi • Managing editor: Julia Wallace
• Production manager: Maggie Hart • Copy editor: Marissa Earl •
Proofreaders: Bailey Utecht, Karissa Silvers

Book design by Kevin Quach

For details on special quantity discounts for bulk purchases,
contact specialmarketscms@penguinrandomhouse.com.

For Benjamin the Owl,
Katelyn the Magpie,
Timothy the Mockingbird,
and Beverly, my adventurous nestmate.

Let no one think it absurd to learn virtue from birds.

—VENERABLE BEDE, C. A.D. 721[1]

FOREWORD

Ask any friend who comes in the morning to get me up in my wheelchair. I love my backyard birds. The chatter of finches, the color of Rufous-sided Towhees, and the flash of feathers around the bird feeder. Birds are the best! And if the feeder gets low on seed, my husband is quick to fill it to the rim. That feeder and a variety of bird books have introduced me to an array of towhees, American Goldfinches, Tufted Titmice, and more.

Friends who know about my fascination with birds are always sending me articles. So, I wasn't surprised when Mike, a pastor-friend in the PCA (Presbyterian Church in America), emailed, "I don't do this often, but I am sending this link out far and wide. Kevin Burrell is a good brother, a PCA pastor, and for what it's worth, a fellow special-needs dad. He has become an eloquent writer on his blog about birds and theology. Take a few minutes and read this latest installment! You will be glad you did."

It was an essay about the Arctic Tern, complete with photos. As I read, I became mesmerized by the strange habits of this extraordinary bird, plus the lessons Kevin wisely drew from it. After I finished the essay, I immediately forwarded it to a batch of friends. I then clicked on the subscribe button to Kevin Burrell's blog, Ornitheology: The Gospel According to Birds.

"Like all creation, the birds have something to say about truth, beauty, and a crazy-creative God," writes Kevin. "I'm convinced that, to remain sane and grounded on this planet, every one of us should make some sort of attentive effort to some aspect of God's creation.... You pick: astronomy, gardening, fungus, whatever. I chose birds."[1]

He is right. And for those who explore the enthralling ways of God in creation, there is a double blessing. We not only find joy and delight in grasping God's creative genius, but we also have the pleasure of glorifying him. In turn, God pours on more joy, and we experience a fresh satisfaction with life.

But *really*. God has something to teach us from a Horned Screamer? The answer is in Job 12:7–9: "But ask the animals, and they will teach you, or the birds in the sky, and they will tell you; or speak to the earth, and it will teach you, or let the fish in the sea inform you. Which of all these does not know that the hand of the LORD has done this?"

Yes, the birds in the sky have something to tell us. I recall when my mother took me to the bird exhibition at the Baltimore Zoo. The aviary was aflutter with squawking, brightly colored creatures. Funny-looking toucans and parakeets galore. She then pointed to the sparrows fluttering in the rafters above us. I was sad that they weren't important enough to be in the caged aviary. But Mother observed that—unlike the parrots tethered with chains—the sparrows were free. Birds *do* have something to say. Even Jesus taught, "Are not two sparrows sold for a penny? Yet not one of them will fall to the ground outside your Father's care" (Matthew 10:29). The lesson? God is trustworthy.

Every creature that exists was especially made by God to reflect a unique aspect of its creator. And in a way, Job 12:7–9 releases Kevin Burrell to be our official guide into the world of feathered creatures. He wants us to appreciate the astounding variety of birds on our planet so that we might praise almighty God, the designer who breathed life into every remarkable species.

No wonder Kevin chose such an impressive title for his book: *Considering Sparrows: What Birds Teach Us About Who We*

Are, Where We're Going, and the Joy of Following Jesus. With a title like that, we can be confident the author is a trusted messenger of the gospel, as well as an expert in bird-ology.

So, I highly commend the book you hold in your hands, not as a thing to beautify your coffee table but as a stellar work to stoke your love for our great creator God, helping you recognize his glory in everything he has made.

Even in the Hoary Puffleg.

—JONI EARECKSON TADA
Joni and Friends International Disability Center
Agoura, California

CONTENTS

Prayer of Preparation

O Christ, use this practice of birdwatching
to refine my vision to more fully see as you see,
to look hard for the unseen and unpraised,
    as you so perfectly modeled for us when you
    admired the widow's secret sacrifice in the
        temple,
    or stooped to the cries of suffering outcasts
        along the road,
    or looked up with love at the desperate tax thief
        perched in a tree,

for I know my own blindness extends well
beyond the birds of my yard.

Let this practice incline my heart
to better see as you see, O Lord,
    my neighbors,
    my family in Christ,
    even my enemies.

Let this avocation of birdwatching
become for me a training ground, tutoring
my thoughts, my heart,
my habits, to more intently see
your love expressed in all the details
of your creation, your world, your people.

—From "A Liturgy for Birdwatching"
by Chris Slaten and Doug McKelvey[1]

PROLOGUE
Why Wise People Birdwatch

This is a book that is best read outside. If that's not feasible, you could at least set up some background nature sounds on your phone and light a forest-scented candle.

If you like to birdwatch, I hope you know that, biblically, you're in good company. Wise people birdwatch. Really—that's in the Bible. First Kings 4 describes the great King Solomon this way: "He spoke about plant life, from the cedar of Lebanon to the hyssop that grows out of walls. He also spoke about animals and birds, reptiles and fish" (verse 33). His perceptive wisdom included biological interest, from impressive cedars to tiny crack-in-the-wall plants. And yes, apparently Solomon birdwatched.

Solomon wasn't the only Bible-birder. The sons of Korah knew the difference between a sparrow and a swallow as they watched birds make nests at the temple entrance (Psalm 84:3). Noah scanned the horizon, and Elijah scanned the Kerith Ravine, looking for ravens, although it's true that both of them had a lot more at stake than just logging a morning list. God challenged Job to pay attention to the ostrich, raven, stork, hawk, and eagle (Job 38–39), and probably also the ibis and the rooster (38:36), if he wanted to gain true wisdom. And of course it was Jesus himself who told us to "look at the birds of the air" (Matthew 6:26) and to "consider the ravens" (Luke 12:24)—both spoken as imperatives, mind you. That might not carry the same weight as "Go and make disciples of all nations"

(Matthew 28:19), but it at least gives the impression of a Savior-sanctioned hobby.

None of these characters in Scripture had a life list or a biology degree, let alone a pair of binoculars. When Jesus calls us to consider the birds, he wants us to understand things like redemptive love, trusting faith, and unshakable hope. Those lessons are the more important points, but Jesus used birds to showcase these greater realities. And so, on my best days, birdwatching is a means to a greater end, a window through which the character of God is illustrated.

All the world's a stage for God's wildly creative ingenuity. But when it comes to birds, we get the sense that perhaps God is showing off, turning the innovation dial up to eleven. After all, he *could* have made one species of bird and called it a day. Instead he overwhelms our global senses with over ten thousand species—everything from tiny hummingbirds and kinglets to the largest birds, like the condor and emu—in one creative breath. Each species turns the prism slightly to show us a different angle of a great God: He makes eagles to show his majesty, songbirds to sing his glory, and pelicans to show that he has quite a sense of humor. To learn, we need simply to go where the birds are—which is not hard, since birds are pretty much everywhere. There's probably one outside your window right now, maybe even looking in, wondering what you're doing with that forest-scented candle.

It would be a sad waste not to pay attention to all this feathered goodness, right? The songwriter Rich Mullins was criticized by some for writing a song called "Here in America" in which he simply sang about the beauty of his country's landscape. He replied, "There are people who think that it's a waste of space to write a song just about America—about how America is a beautiful place to live. But I think it's a waste of eyes not to notice."[1] That bird outside your window right now would concur.

Author Dale Ralph Davis explains, "Since God has left the fingerprints of his wisdom everywhere, since there is no place where God does not furnish us with raw materials for godly thinking, Christians should be seized with a rambunctious curiosity to ponder his works, both the majestic and the mundane."[2]

I love that phrase: "rambunctious curiosity." It explains how this book came about in the first place.

Ornitheology Explained

The term *ornitheology* isn't original to me; the word was coined by the famed theologian-birder John Stott in his book *The Birds, Our Teachers.* It's a great description of the interplay between creational attentiveness and biblical teaching, or specifically, the study of birds and the study of God. Although both of those undertakings have been a regular part of my life, they took on new meaning on my front porch swing in the spring of 2020. As a pandemic ruptured our normal routines and forced us to work from home, the porch became the location where I had two necessary ingredients of the field of ornitheology: less hurry and more birds. The birds in my maple tree provided the soundtrack for my devotions and study, and gave me a more grounded sense of time and space. Eventually I found myself writing a couple of articles about the birds in my neighborhood and the lessons they brought to mind. Things developed from there, with follow-ups on species beyond my own locale. Vestiges of my long-discarded undergrad biology degree seemed to find new life as metaphors of the Christian journey.

There are far more knowledgeable ornithologists and far more faithful theologians in this world. But getting to pull these two fields into something new has been a fulfilling undertaking as an attempt to encourage the bird-curious Christian and the faith-curious birder. Along the way, I've been grateful for the people who have appreciated Ornitheology.com and have encouraged me to put some bird thoughts together into a book. But how to approach the task?

As a pastor, my preferred approach to preaching has always been to walk through a book of the Bible verse by verse, taking it in sections that connect the passages together into a faithful whole. Although the blog has mostly featured a random assortment of topics connected to a random assortment of birds, I wondered what it might be like to apply my preaching method and write my way through a book of the Bible "in bird." This book is an attempt to live that conviction; think of it as "expository birdwatching."

I chose the book dearest to me, Paul's letter to the Philippians. In Philippians, a short New Testament letter to Europe's first church, the congregation is healthy, the spotlight is Jesus, and the tone is joy, despite the fact that its author wrote the whole thing from prison. We should be all-ears attentive when someone writes from a jail cell; words born from chains carry added weight.

If you're hoping for a commentary, you'll be disappointed, although it's my hope that you'll know the book of Philippians better as a result of this exercise. If you're hoping for a devotional, that might be closer to the point, although it's a little heavy on the zoology. To strike the balance, I've committed to not getting preachy for too long without bringing it back to birds and not getting too bird-detailed without bringing it back to the Bible.

Secrets and Disclaimers

If you're not a birdwatcher, let me tell you a secret about this book: It's really not about birds. Pastors live in the world of sermon illustrations, always looking for embedded truth in everything around them. We tell jokes, to the groans of the flock. We tell stories about our kids, to their horror. We share military stories and music lyrics and Pixar clips and C. S. Lewis quotes (oh yes, especially C. S. Lewis quotes), all in an attempt to somehow extol the greatest story—one that begins and ends in a bird-filled garden. All truth is God's truth, good stories tell the great story, and every corner of God's creation is a window to the gospel if we have the eyes to see it. Think of these chapters as a collection of extended sermon illustrations. With feathers.

If you *are* a birdwatcher, I have a secret for you as well: The most important parts of this book are not the birdy parts. The Lord can use something we are passionate about (like birds) to grow in us a greater passion for him. The signpost is not the destination, but it points there.

Anything worth writing should come with disclaimers, and I offer two. First, in the pages that follow, I will unashamedly anthropomorphize birds. I want to find places where their world feels like ours, and so I'll often attribute motives, emotions, abstract thinking, evil intent (I'm looking at you, cowbirds), and enough scientific faux pas to make a zoologist cringe. But for the purposes of the book, it's a lot more fun that way, and I'd encourage you to just go with it.

Second, I want to make my intentions clear up front: The purpose of every chapter I write is to point you to the completed work of Jesus. For some, that might feel too preachy for a book about birds. But remember, it's not *really* a book about birds. Rather, it's a book about the grander realities of how a life is defined by something Christians simply call "the gospel." *Gospel* means "good news," and that's a crucial definition for anyone who wants to understand the difference between Christianity and any other religious or philosophical system. Good news is not good advice or good morals or good steps to a healthy marriage. Words like those don't have power to *create* life; they only have power to *advise* it, and then *we* have to do the work and achieve the outcomes. But good news is vastly different. It isn't something we do; it's something we *receive.* We can approach religion as a framework that tells us what we need to do to get to God, or we can approach it in the uniquely Christian way of responding to what God has already done to get to us. How the life, death, and resurrection of Jesus does that will, I hope, be apparent in these musings.

There has been much written on the book of Philippians that will frame these pages, but I believe this is the first that comes with the exhortation to light a forest-scented candle.

A Brief Note About Bird References

A good name is more desirable than great riches.

—PROVERBS 22:1

Two brief comments are in order for the various bird names referenced in the pages ahead.

First, bird names are in a constant state of flux. As one of the bigger examples, the American Ornithological Society (the organization that standardizes all bird names) announced in November 2023 that it would be changing the English names of all North American birds that have been named after a person. This decision affects 152 of the continent's 1,100-plus species—more than one in ten. A lengthy (and probably contentious) renaming process lies ahead, and so it's possible that some of the birds mentioned in this book have a different name by the time you read this. Honestly, though, this is nothing new; species are constantly being re-sorted, reclassified, and renamed. Even classic works like John James Audubon's *The Birds of America* were already out-of-date before they reached printers. Meanwhile, while ornithologists wrestle for the perfect name, the birds go about their lives, business as usual, presumably calling each other whatever they feel like.

I explain all this to say, the names used in this book were the common parlance as of the date of publication, and a quick

Google search should connect the dots for you if a name seems unfamiliar.

The second comment refers to my use of capital letters when naming birds. The common (though not universal) practice in the United States is to capitalize the common English name of a species. At times this may feel a bit weird. For instance, there are lots of yellow warblers, but there's also a species called a Yellow Warbler. Most jays have some blue on them, but there's only one Blue Jay. Kenn Kaufman writes, "Readers unfamiliar with birding or ornithology may find all these capital letters jarring at first, but they help bring clarity when we're discussing the roughly eleven thousand known species of birds."[1] So when I write about a goldfinch, we'll keep things informally lowercase, but when I refer to an American Goldfinch, we'll give the proper noun its due. Hopefully you'll get used to it.

Let's start with the difference between a parrot and a Mealy Parrot . . .

CONSIDERING SPARROWS

— CHAPTER 1 —

The Caged Bird Sings

It has become clear throughout the whole palace guard and to everyone else that I am in chains for Christ.

—PHILIPPIANS 1:13

The soul helps the body, and at certain moments uplifts it. It is the only bird which sustains its cage.

—VICTOR HUGO[1]

DOES A CAGED bird count?

In the unspoken rules of "life list" birding, convictions may vary. A life list, as the words imply, is a list of every bird a person has identified in their life to date. Birders keep scads of lists: year lists, county lists, state lists, patch lists, yard lists. But there is one list to rule them all: the life list. To add a bird to your life list—to see a bird that you've *never* seen before—well, that's a really good day.

There is no agreed-upon set of varsity-league birding rules for life lists, so birders tend to let their conscience guide them. The purists only count birds they've identified visually. The artists only count birds they've photographed. Regular-type birders like myself are usually willing to make do with any sort of ID, sight or song, so long as it's definitive, making it a lot easier to bag those owls and whip-poor-wills. But there's one thing all serious birders agree on.

Zoos don't count.

And thus my dilemma. I was on a day trip with some friends in the Panamanian rainforest, enjoying an afternoon of canopy zip-lining. I had honestly expected to spot some birds along the way, but the Panamanian canopy is surprisingly quiet in the heat of the afternoon, and more concentration was required for jumping out of trees than I anticipated. Thus far the day was a ten on the fun meter but a bust on birding.

As we turned in our gear and helmets and walked a dusty street to some nearby shops, I heard the clarion call of a parrot. I scanned the trees and followed the sound, turning into an alley between two shops. Lo and behold, there it was: a gorgeous bright-green Mealy Parrot[2]—a bird not previously on any of my lists. A lifer!

Did I mention it was in a cage?

The large square metal cage sat on a wooden bench in the

alley, with a youngish boy sitting next to it. The parrot jabbered cheerfully, as if he and the boy were having a casual conversation. A lifer, yes, but cages sure feel like cheating. Does a caged bird count? To reiterate, I had spent the day in the canopy of a *rainforest*—supposedly the pinnacle of biodiversity—and all I had to show for it was one semi-cooperative Crowned Woodnymph on the approach trail. The birds of Panama are not to be taken for granted, apparently. And here was a lifer, right in front of me and clearly not going anywhere.

In broken Spanish, I asked the boy tending the cage where he got the bird. He assured me he had just captured the parrot that week, and pointed to the nearby tree from which he had nabbed it. Ahhh, a local! If I'd been under that tree just last week, it would have counted. The bird could practically see his old apartment from here.

Today the Mealy Parrot sits on my list as Bird #275. Don't judge me.

A Church Founded on a Prison Break

The apostle Paul wants the Philippians to know that a caged bird still counts. Stuck in a prison most likely in Rome,[3] Paul isn't in the most idyllic place to pen a letter; authors today probably would prefer a mountain retreat or beach bungalow for pursuing their creative muse. Furthermore, prison is a definite liability for a man called to be a world traveler for the gospel. I mean, the back of your Bible needs at least four maps just to describe all the places Paul went. Imagine God calling you to take a message to the nations only to be locked in a cell. Wouldn't you wonder if you'd misunderstood the assignment? Metaphorically, Paul's wings have been clipped.

We might expect Paul to lament his circumstances. "I'm done. I've been benched. My disciple-making days are over."

But there's no hint of sour grapes or second-guessing. In fact, Paul radiates encouragement and positivity in this letter. The tone of Philippians—beginning to end—is inexplicable joy. William Blake once asked, "How can the bird that is born for joy sit in a cage and sing?"[4] It doesn't make sense to us. But then again, it *does,* in part because Paul hasn't forgotten the origin story of the Philippian church—a story that also prominently features a prison cell. Remember how the church at Philippi—the first Christian church in Europe—got its start?

Acts 16 tells the story. Lydia, the first convert in the region, gave Paul and company a home base from which to meet. However, their second convert gave them an audience, and not necessarily a friendly one; a miraculous exorcism freed a slave girl, but the subsequent loss of her dark-arts business enraged her handlers. And so Paul and his partner Silas, deemed a threat to the city, were beaten repeatedly with rods, sent to an inner cell (in other words, no windows), and fastened to the stocks by their feet. Welcome to European church planting, Paul.

Just hours later, however, they found themselves in their newly baptized jailer's living room with a home-cooked meal for their stomachs and salve for their wounds. What happened between Scene A and Scene B? What started with some harmless singing ended with a scene measurable on the Richter scale: "Suddenly there was such a violent earthquake that the foundations of the prison were shaken. At once all the prison doors flew open, and everyone's chains came loose" (Acts 16:26).

Apparently, the Lord is not confined by cages.

Years later, when Paul writes to the Philippians from his latest prison Vrbo, his Philippian jailer friend is likely one of the recipients. Imagine him smiling as Paul's letter is read out loud to the gathered congregation: "Whether I am in chains or defending and confirming the gospel, all of you share in God's grace with me" (Philippians 1:7). The jailer nods knowingly. He knows the gospel still sings in a prison cell and that when God is good and ready, locked doors will shake once more and release Paul for his next assignment. Right now, however, God has work for Paul to do in jail.

Sometimes God opens prison doors. Other times he works through closed ones. Paul speaks of how the whole palace guard—a captive audience—is hearing about Christ:

> What has happened to me has actually served to advance the gospel. As a result, it has become clear throughout the whole palace guard and to everyone else that I am in chains for Christ. And because of my chains, most of the brothers and sisters have become confident in the Lord and dare all the more to proclaim the gospel without fear. (Philippians 1:12–14)

Paul's cage doesn't impede his witness; it *amplifies* it. Prison unleashes his song. It brings the message up close where the palace guard and all the other neighbors can see it, hear it, and by God's grace, understand it.

A Cage-Enabled Song

My earliest childhood memory of a bird wasn't even a bird at all. Just a couple of doors down from our tiny house in East Rochester, New York, sat an equally tiny house occupied by an elderly widow named Katherine. My mother and I would often stop by to visit. As a four-year-old instantly bored by adult conversation, what excited me about Katherine's house was her bird. It perched on a swing in a small, round metal cage, a bird-shaped housing of gears and feathers in the form of a small white canary. When we wound up the crank on the back of the cage, it would swing on its perch and sing a thin, tin-sounding canary song. It was a glorified music box, but I was mesmerized. As my mother chatted with Katherine, I would turn the silver crank on the back of the cage again and again, reactivating the joyous song of the bird inside. Without the crank on the cage, the bird would sit inert; it was *the cage itself* that enabled the song.

I said before that for the birder, zoos are life-list taboo. But just because I don't log them in my journal doesn't mean I'm not enthralled by a good zoo aviary. Yes, I know zoos are controversial institutions, and you may be one who has strong opinions against any form of animal captivity. After all, there are an estimated ten thousand zoos in this world, and certainly some are less humane than others. Still, it can't be denied that the best zoos incite wonder. An aviary brings distant birds close enough for us to be captivated by them. The colors of another world infiltrate ours.

God does this with Paul. Throughout his two-year imprisonment in Rome, he wears a chain about eighteen inches long, on the other end of which sits a no-nonsense Praetorian soldier. These soldiers rotate through his day in four-to-six-hour shifts, twenty-four seven. We can presume that several dozen soldiers will take their turn at the other end of Paul's chain during the span of his incarceration. God fetters them eighteen inches from the gospel. From heaven's perspective, Paul isn't chained to these soldiers; *they* are chained to *him*—a captive audience. New life radiates from Paul's cell, all the way to the palace itself; when Paul says at the end of his letter, "All God's people here send you greetings, especially those who belong to Caesar's household" (Philippians 4:22), it speaks of a subversive revolution, that people inside Caesar's own home are embracing the gospel.

Paul could never have had that sort of access as a free man, but faith-transformed soldiers are contagious. Rome is at the center of the empire, the palace is at the center of Rome, and inside the palace itself, the gospel advances unchained. Paul is exactly where he's supposed to be, inciting wonder. The difficulties of Paul's confinement are also the whispers of another world, a message brought near for his captors and visitors to hear.

God is still doing this with us. It's in the challenges of life—the confinements, the damp cell of our circumstances—that the gospel has an opportunity to shine for the benefit of those around us. If you've ever browsed at a jewelry store, you know the finest diamonds are displayed over black velvet. Every jeweler knows a treasure shines brightest against a dark background.

What about you? Does the dark background of a difficult situation steal your song or activate it? Paul's joyous attitude as a convict is probably hard to swallow for most of us. We don't easily filter our difficulties through the lens of joy. A few sentences later, Paul writes, "For it has been granted to you on behalf of Christ not only to believe in him, but also to suffer for him, since you are going through the same struggle you saw I had, and now hear that I still have" (Philippians 1:29–30). The *opportunity* of suffering? Usually that's not the first thought that comes to mind when we're in the pit. But what aspects of your cell might be hard providence for the sake of communicating gospel realities—to you and to those around you? When life feels like a cage, what if that's the moment to turn the crank and activate your song?

God does some of his best work in cages. Should we be surprised? Our faith is built on it. The most confining moment of Jesus's life secured our freedom. His brief imprisonment moved swiftly to the crushing limitations of crucifixion. No one on a Roman cross was expected to accomplish anything, and yet in those moments, Jesus accomplished *everything*. Like jewelry, this treasure shines brightest against a dark background.

Following *that* kind of savior doesn't promise us a life of ease. We have prisons to visit and cold, stony places to sit in. When we walk in his steps, they sometimes lead us into valley-of-the-shadow-of-death scenarios. But God reveals himself—to us and others—in those places. "Because of this I rejoice. Yes, and I will continue to rejoice" (Philippians 1:18).

The Cross of Jesus is proof positive that God does some of his best work in cages. Taking comfort in that, how might you embrace the Lord's work even when the light struggles to break through? How might your cell be your stage to magnify your Savior?

— CHAPTER 2 —

Albatross Commitment

Being confident of this, that he who began a good work in you will carry it on to completion until the day of Christ Jesus.

—PHILIPPIANS 1:6

Child of God, you cost Christ too much for him to forget you.

—CHARLES H. SPURGEON[1]

"WHERE CAN WISDOM be found?" asks Job 28:12. Answer: Midway Atoll in Hawaii, at least during breeding season.

Wisdom—in the non-Socratic sense—is the name of a Laysan Albatross whom researchers have dubbed the world's oldest known wild bird. First banded by scientists in 1956, and having already laid an egg (something albatrosses don't do before age five), Wisdom is at least seventy-four years old at the time of this writing. Job 12:12 asks, "Is not wisdom found among the aged?" Yes indeed, Job.

Laysan Albatrosses are renowned for their committed lifelong monogamy, so when Wisdom's partner Akeakamai (clever: it's Hawaiian for "lover of wisdom") didn't show up at the breeding grounds in 2021, and again in 2022, it became apparent that Wisdom had outlived her mate—a sixty-year partnership.[2] Imagine that. These two birds had been an item since the first days of Beatlemania, a young and carefree couple setting out on the ocean blue, the world as their oyster. For sixty years they toured the North Pacific, swinging back to Hawaii regularly for another nesting season. In their lifetime, they cared for fifty to sixty eggs and raised over thirty chicks to adulthood. At their diamond anniversary party, Akeakamai would stare into his beloved's eyes and quote Ecclesiastes 2:9: "In all this my wisdom stayed with me."

Albatrosses are willing to commit—a quality that's especially showcased in their dating years. The initial days of a potential partnership are marked by "pair-bonding," a ritual that's generally recognized as the most elaborate courtship in the bird world. The behavior looks a bit like a modern dance class, with postures that are given names like "the bob-strut," "the clapper," "the sky moo," and "the stare." Honestly, any of these could be the next Macarena. In sequence, these pseudo-yoga poses give the effect of a highly choreographed performance, obsessively repeated for hours, days, months, even *years*. In fact, the pair-bonding stage of the relationship can go on for up to three breeding seasons before the birds finally decide to consummate the relationship. You can't hurry love.

This prolonged engagement lays the foundation for an admirably committed life together. But don't be fooled by the picture-perfect relationship at their vacation home in Hawaii. For an albatross, their *real* home is the sea, and in that realm they travel solo.

Loosely Monogamous

While the Laysan Albatross is a commendable example of commitment, other species deserve honorable mentions as well. Lovebirds are an obvious contender, with their habit of sitting together for long stretches, staring into each other's eyes. The Sandhill Crane is another laudable example; my in-laws' Florida backyard has given us years of opportunity to observe the daily behaviors of a loving and committed family. Scarlet Macaws are famously committed; I observed an odd-numbered flock firsthand on a trip to Costa Rica, and our guide noted that this meant one of them was either a juvenile or, more likely, a widow. Bald Eagles and Atlantic Puffins also mate for life, along with condors, Black Vultures, and loads of waterfowl. Perhaps the king of commitment is the Bewick's Swan. Researchers in England have studied this species for over fifty years without finding a single case of "bird divorce" among thousands of parenting pairs.

But all that faithfulness aside, a bird relationship isn't always as devoted as it sounds. In a college zoology class, I learned that 90 percent of bird species are monogamous. It turns out that this statement was overly optimistic, or at least overly romanticized. "Monogamous"—in the biological sense of the term—is best defined as "having one mate at a time." By that definition, yes, most birds are monogamous (with rare exceptions like those philandering hummingbirds). But we too easily sentimentalize that.

First, it's not about mating for life. In fact, a majority of birds remain faithful to their mate for the current nesting season but are just as likely to find a new partner the following spring (yes, sort of like college students). Thus many birds aren't as intent on finding Mr. or Mrs. Right as much as Mr. or Mrs. Right Now. They're faithful but not *enduring.* True, this meets the technical definition of biological monogamy, but it's probably not the picture you had in mind. In fact, with newer DNA technologies, scientists are now discovering that birds aren't quite as faithful as we imagined. Let's just say it's possible that not all the eggs in the nest belong to Daddy.

Second, it's not about building a life together. A commitment to build a nest, incubate an egg for two months, and co-parent a chick is a beautiful partnership. But it doesn't come with the expectation of weekly coffee dates and deep conversation. I suppose I pictured Wisdom soaring wing tip to wing tip across the Pacific with her hubby on a romantic island tour in the offseason. They would learn each other's Enneagram numbers and love languages and laugh over espressos in exotic cafés. But it turns out that albatrosses are famously solitary outside of the breeding season, so much so that one species is called the Wandering Albatross. (*Wandering* is not a word that's the key to a thriving marriage.) For an albatross, *monogamous* means "Hey, it was fun. So, see you next year?" Then it's off and away for nine months of me time. We will never know what happened to Wisdom's mate . . . and neither will Wisdom. She wasn't there when it happened. And since then, she's apparently moved on, bob-strutting and sky-mooing with a new partner, and even laying another egg in 2024.[3]

I know that's a heavy dose of reality to pour on the flames of our budding bird romance imagery. But it prepares us to consider a far deeper faithfulness and a far more beautiful commitment.

Horizontal and Vertical Faithfulness

In Philippians, we're invited to eavesdrop on a faithful partnership in progress. Paul's opening salutation commends the Philippians for their steadfast commitment. "I thank my God every time I remember you. In all my prayers for all of you, I always pray with joy because of your partnership in the gospel from the first day until now" (Philippians 1:3–5). The rest of the letter evidences this. This church has shared with Paul in God's grace (1:7), given sacrificially (4:14–16), and even sent a messenger who almost died to deliver their letter and extend their care (2:30). To Paul, the Philippians are evidence of God at work, a reminder that his efforts are not in vain (2:16). They have contended by his side through some of his hardest moments (4:3).

Paul reciprocates with the sorts of words and phrases we reserve for our closest friends. And he's lavish with them: Paul describes his heart-level affection for the Philippians (1:7), a longing to reunite (1:8), a willingness to stave off death for the sake of their growth (1:24–25) and be poured out as a drink offering for the sake of their faith (2:17), and a desire to fuel their confidence in Christ (1:26). Paul and the Philippians have a wing-tip-to-wing-tip partnership, overflowing with the language and pathos of faithful commitment.

But what really inspires Paul isn't the horizontal commitment but the vertical one. As enduring as this church-and-missionary partnership is, it pales in comparison with the grip of grace—the unrelenting love of a tenacious God: "Being confident of this, that he who began a good work in you will carry it on to completion until the day of Christ Jesus" (Philippians 1:6).

Put simply, God finishes what he starts. My home, sadly, is full of the debris of half-finished undertakings: projects that failed to stay in budget, repairs that failed to stay within the scope of my limited know-how, or ideas that simply failed to sustain my interest. For whatever reason—lack of time, funding, focus, or expertise—the work still sits uncompleted. It's fair to say that each abandoned task began with good intentions. But all of them fell victim to the limitations of, well, *me.*

God has no such limitations. The will of God is never limited by the capacity of God. He can do whatever he wants, and what he *wants* (among other things) is for his people to remain secure in his grip: "I give them eternal life, and they shall never perish; no one will snatch them out of my hand" (John 10:28).

God does not let go. The pair-bond is ironclad. This confidence, despite the faith and faithfulness of the Philippians, isn't rooted in their commitments and competencies. It isn't for us either. Honestly, if this relationship was up to us, we wouldn't have much reason to expect a happy ending.

Thankfully, God knows this and planned accordingly.

Unilateral Commitment

If albatross commitment is sealed with the complexities of dance, consider the greater reality of God's commitment to us. Abraham is my favorite example of this. God intended to create a nation through him—an ambitious task for a crew of three: Abram, Sarah, and their nephew Lot. (True, they didn't have a lot, but they did have a guy named Lot.) By Genesis 15, ten years have passed, and this nation-building team has not only *not* increased but has actually *decreased* by 33 percent, with Lot choosing to seek his fortune in a seemed-like-a-good-idea-at-the-time city called Sodom. When God appears to Abram/Abraham again, it makes sense that this eighty-five-year-old nomad asks, "Sovereign LORD, how can I know that I will gain possession of it?" (Genesis 15:8).

God's answer? "Bring me a heifer, a goat and a ram, each three years old, along with a dove and a young pigeon" (Genesis 15:9). If you were praying and asking God for an answer and he responded with a list of livestock and birds, you'd likely be a little confused. This answer confounds our twenty-first-century ears. But it wasn't confusing to Abraham, because these moves were all part of the partnership postures and poses of an ancient Near Eastern treaty.

Drafting up a legal agreement at that time lacked the familiar sights of lawyers, notaries, and closing documents. Instead, two parties would sacrifice animals and splay the parts on two sides of a path. Then the participants would walk between. It was referred to as *karat berit*—"cutting a covenant"—and if practiced today would doubtless make the office a bit more lively the next time you refinance a mortgage. The symbolic act of walking between the bloody pieces called down a self-incriminating curse. The first person would walk the gauntlet, signifying, "If I fail to keep my end of this agreement, may what happened to these animals happen to me." The second person would follow suit—usually, at least. But the greater the disparity in rank and power between the two parties, the less obliged the greater one might be to call down a curse upon himself. After all, he's holding all the cards and can enact vows without lowering himself to make them. So often the higher-ranking party sits this pair-bonding dance out and lets the vassal do all the bob-strutting and sky-mooing by himself.[4]

Abraham understands all these customs and dutifully splays out the pieces. But clearly God holds all the cards in this scene, and Abraham would rightly expect the oath swearing and curse calling to fall solely on him. He awaits the command to walk between the pieces. Surprisingly, it never comes.

The shock of this story comes in the form of, as best as we can translate it, a blazing torch and a smoking firepot, two mysterious symbols. We strain our imagination trying to picture this scene, but for the ancient Israelites first hearing this story, both words would have been familiar—the same words that described what Israel saw in their desert wanderings. The firepot and the torch are two manifestations of God's presence, a callback to the pillar of cloud by day and the pillar of fire by night, guiding Israel daily through their journeys. And here they *both* are, floating between the animal pieces, sealing this agreement for *both* sides: "Abraham, if I fail this partnership, may what happened to these animals happen to me. But if *you* fail this partnership, I say it again: May what happened to these animals happen to *me*." Abraham is relegated to the role of spectator and is never asked to walk the gauntlet, because God does it, *twice*. He doesn't enact a vow *from* Abraham but makes a vow *to* him:

"Abraham, when *you* break the covenant, *I* will die."

There simply is no commitment that compares with this commitment. By comparison, all the greatest examples of monogamy—bird or human—could fill a thimble and still have room for the thumb. God locks arms with his people and doesn't let go. This partnership has nothing to do with our faithfulness, good intentions, or inherent awesomeness. Let's be gut-honest: If the story of the Bible was based on our commitment to God, it would only be three chapters thick. It reads much better as the story of his commitment to us.

God makes good on the agreement. A few hundred years later, Isaiah prophesied about Jesus, saying: "He was cut off from the land of the living" (Isaiah 53:8). The language here is explicitly covenantal, hearkening back to the *karat berit*. He was cut off—cursed—not because he failed his end of the deal but because we failed ours and he said, "I'll pay it." When *you* fail, *I* die. That's what it required for him to keep holding us in the grip of grace.

My faith tradition often cites a doctrine referred to as "the perseverance of the saints"—the assurance that God won't abandon the work of his saving hands but promises to finish what he started. I love the promise, but the wording gives us too much credit. My life is a testimony to radically inconsistent perseverance: brief moments of nest-keeping obedience punctuated with long stretches soaring alone at sea. Prone to wander, Lord, I feel it—prone to wander like a Wandering Albatross.

Mercifully, our final hope isn't grounded in our perseverance with God but in God's perseverance with us. Through our failure and rebellion, God traces a consistent story of persevering love all the way to a cross that says, to his first disciples and to us: "Having loved his own who were in the world, he loved them to the end" (John 13:1). Beyond the grave, and to the final throne, he remains just as faithful.

I recommend we forever rename the doctrine to "the perseverance of *God with* the saints." After all, he's the consistent one, not me. He never lets go. Never gives up. It is his grip, and his alone, that gives us confidence that "he who began a good work in you will carry it on to completion until the day of Christ Jesus" (Philippians 1:6). Or as the old hymn assures:

> The work which His goodness began,
> the arm of His strength will complete;
> His promise is yea and amen,
> and never was forfeited yet.
> Things future, nor things that are now,
> nor all things below or above,
> can make Him His purpose forgo,
> or sever my soul from His love.[5]

— CHAPTER 3 —

The Empty Nest

This is my prayer: that your love may abound more and more in knowledge and depth of insight, so that you may be able to discern what is best and may be pure and blameless for the day of Christ, filled with the fruit of righteousness that comes through Jesus Christ—to the glory and praise of God.

—PHILIPPIANS 1:9–11

It may be hard for an egg to turn into a bird: it would be a jolly sight harder for it to learn to fly while remaining an egg. We are like eggs at present. And you cannot go on indefinitely being just an ordinary, decent egg. We must be hatched or go bad.

—C. S. LEWIS[1]

IT'S THE QUESTION every parent of a basement-dwelling, video-game-playing thirtysomething has asked. What is a reasonable expectation for when a child should "leave the nest"?

There's probably no one-size-fits-all answer, owing to the unique variables of family dynamics, cultural differences, financial realities, and personal abilities or disabilities. Some parents set their expectations too soon; I remember a well-known pastor describing the moment, at age sixteen, when his father sent him off for the summer with some cash, a train ticket to Colorado, and the instructions, "Figure it out."

More often, parents set their expectations too low, not sure how to walk the fine line between supportiveness and coddling. It's yet another season of *The Simpsons,* where Bart, Lisa, and Baby Maggie have been living at home in a state of arrested development since 1989.

Both extremes, and a whole lot in the middle, are featured in the bird world. Nesting strategies vary significantly, and we'll look at the different approaches in a moment. But it's best to start with the *why.* For what purpose is a bird hatched into this world? And for humans like us, to what purpose were *we* hatched?

One expansive description of that purpose is found in Philippians 1:9–11—by far one of my favorite passages of Scripture. I pronounce it as a prayer at weddings and ordination services, and as a benediction to my congregation every Sunday morning. I lift my arms as a symbolic laying on of hands and recite these words as a blessing over the assembled saints, scanning the room to look as many of them in the eye as I can. These words are the promise I want to see fulfilled in the people I love. Here they are:

> This is my prayer: that your love may abound more and more in knowledge and depth of insight, so that you may

> be able to discern what is best and may be pure and blameless for the day of Christ, filled with the fruit of righteousness that comes through Jesus Christ—to the glory and praise of God.

In essence, I'm praying for their growth, for their maturity in the faith, for the Lord to grow them to more and more reflect the image of Christ. I'm praying that the hatched egg of their faith would develop and "fledge" into what they were gloriously made for. This is the goal of a disciple: growth in knowledge, discernment, holiness, and a capacity to bear fruit. Consider some of the people you've spiritually invested in over the years. Don't you long to see these qualities in them? Don't you long to see them in *yourself* as well? We take joy in watching people "grow up" into these things.

But how does it happen, and what does it look like?

Nest Investments

If you're a bird, there are two basic strategies for getting your chicks from egg to independent living: precocial and altricial. Precocial birds start their lives as if fired from a cannon. They're already capable of a lot of adulty things like walking and running or even swimming and flying, without wasting a lot of time on the Wonder Years. Quail, for instance, hit the ground running—literally. Kiwi can immediately find food without any lessons from mom and dad. And ducklings take to the water like—well, like a duck to water.

Perhaps the most extreme example of the precocial strategy is the Malleefowl (and related scrubfowl) of Australia—so overachieving that scientists have dubbed them "superprecocial." The eggs are incubated in a huge pile of dirt and debris, and when the chicks hatch, they have to dig their way out, a process taking up to fifteen hours, without a parent or legal guardian anywhere in the vicinity. When they finally emerge from the ground, having already had some time to experience the harsh realities of life, they freeze in place for a solid twenty minutes (PTSD does that to you), then gather up their courage and wander off to face the cruel world, entirely alone. Happy birthday, champ.

Or there's the Torrent Duck of Chile. Although it has the longest incubation period of any waterfowl—around forty-four days—that extra time in the oven makes for a rude awakening upon hatching, with a rite of passage that David Attenborough calls "so dramatic it seems almost suicidal."[2] The duckling's first act is to cannonball off a cliff into the cold, raging torrent (thus the name). This might win the award for the most abrupt empty-nest experience imaginable.

Or perhaps that award should go to the Hooded Merganser, a widespread North American duck. Jumping into water is child's play by comparison. Mergansers nest in tree cavities up to fifty feet off the ground, and when the chicks hatch, they'll need to climb out of the hollow and then get up the guts to take a Mission: Impossible–style jump to the hard ground below. You really should set down this book for a moment and google this. It's great in slow motion, and yes, they bounce. Go ahead, I'll wait.[3]

Unlike these precocial birds, altricial birds come into the world with few advantages and low expectations. Featherless, sightless, helpless, clueless—they look less like a bird and more like a dog's rubber chew toy. It's difficult to imagine that one day they'll have the sharp coloring of a Western Tanager or a Cape May Warbler when they start off looking more like the eraser end of a pencil. These youngsters will need some work.

Altricial parenting is not for the weak. Since chicks can't feed themselves, the job falls to a quickly exhausted mom and dad. A songbird chick can eat its own body weight in food every day, which makes the grocery bill challenging already. But now factor in that they're feeding triplets, quadruplets, or even quintuplets, and it's no surprise that parents are *constantly* foraging, making trips to the nest every fifteen minutes, twelve to fourteen hours a day, without any me time. A Great Tit, for instance, may deliver over nine hundred beakfuls of insects a day to the greedy little mouths back at the nest. That's why altricial parents tend to lay fewer eggs; after all, life's going to get bonkers when it's time to feed that brood, so why make it harder on yourself?

I'm oversimplifying a bit. Biologists also refer to semi-precocial birds, semi-altricial birds, and even different levels of precociality.[4] Not all precocial birds are deadbeat parents (Sandhill Cranes mentor their young for up to ten months), and not all altricial chicks take it slow and easy (Lapland Longspurs fledge in just twelve days because the parents are able to feed their young more abundantly in perpetual daylight). But these are the two options, generally speaking.

There are pros and cons to each approach. Precocial birds (about 20 percent of all species) get an adrenaline-fueled start, but their brain development tapers off later on. Altricial birds, on the other hand, might start slowly, but the parents deliver a steady supply of high-protein food, so their brains grow steadily to a proportionately larger size than precocial birds'. In essence, it's the tortoise and the hare, or as Jennifer Ackerman writes, "Nest sitters end up with bigger brains than nest quitters."[5] It's a trade-off. Do we want greater expectations from the starting gate, or do we want to take the long view?

For a Christ-follower seeking to grow toward spiritual maturity, the answer must be both.

Hatched for a Purpose

When it comes to fledging a new believer from the nest, churches and ministries can easily err at the extremes.

If we lean in the "precocial" direction, we'll focus on hatching at the expense of development—in other words, evangelism at the expense of discipleship. The presumption (usually unspoken) is that a new believer instantly has all the capacities of a mature believer, so if we can lead a person to make a decision for Christ, the Holy Spirit will take it from there. It's assumed this newly hatched life will instinctively know how to feed itself on Scripture, pray, and find healthy community in a local church. Instead, various studies suggest that less than 15 percent of those who profess faith at a crusade become actively involved in a church one year later.[6]

Just to be clear, I'm not one to belittle the effectiveness of a crusade. Living in North Carolina, I often take visiting pastors, missionaries, and friends to the Billy Graham Library here in Charlotte. I've walked the exhibits and displays enough times to feel the massive impact of a life of proclamation, and the people I bring often have stories of their own. *I was at the 1953 St. Louis Crusade—that's where life truly began for me.* Or, *I remember when this crusade came behind the Iron Curtain to my country and gave hope to my mother, who passed it on to us.* If only 15 percent of the 2.2 million professions of faith at Billy Graham Crusades bore lasting fruit, that's still astounding. True conversion finds its way. The Holy Spirit guides Christians through those early lessons, and we aren't left alone to dig ourselves out of the dirt. But biblically, the Spirit seems to love using the ministry of other believers to chart the path of discipleship—something Billy Graham's team saw when they began connecting new believers with local churches. Our fledging strategy can't end at the commitment card.

So when a person becomes a Christian, we don't want to adopt the precocial "figure it out" method. But we don't want to accept an altricial strategy either. It's far too easy for seasoned believers to view a new believer as a helpless chick, relegated to the nest until they can open their eyes and earn a few feathers.

Before we let them out in public, we require them to complete our discipleship curriculum, sort out the incongruous aspects of their lifestyle, attend our membership class, and maybe memorize some catechism—all within the safety bubble of the nest. It's rarely stated this strongly, of course, but that doesn't mean the attitude isn't widespread. Rookies belong on the bench, right? We contemplate all the important things new believers need to learn, but we fail to get them in the game.

New Christians don't need three years of seminary before they can serve the kingdom. While there are some helpful guidelines in Scripture that keep us from throwing someone too quickly into the white water (like 1 Timothy 5:22: "Do not be hasty in the laying on of hands"), we're also shown how quickly a convert can make a difference. The Philippian church was full of such examples, like the jailer who introduced his household to Christ (Acts 16:34) or Lydia, who offered her home to other believers within minutes of her conversion (Acts 16:15). Ask yourself, "Where can I encourage new faith to participate in kingdom work?" In my own experience, new believers strengthen the rest of the congregation with a refreshing vibrancy. Their questions and excitement may inspire seasoned believers to rediscover truths that they had begun to take for granted.

Wherever you are in your walk with the Lord, how do you view your potential? You may be a seasoned believer who needs to *start* a Bible study, not just sign up for another one. Or you may be relatively new to faith, a little overwhelmed by the awareness of everything you don't know yet. At any place along that continuum, you may be tempted to think true spiritual maturity is something for ministers, missionaries, and monks. Leave the work to the "trained professionals" and stay safely in the nest. But as an adopted child of God, you aren't relegated to the junior varsity team. You're varsity, folks. When Paul prays for the Philippians' deepening knowledge, discernment, purity, blamelessness, and abounding fruit, that prayer is for you too. To what purposes has God hatched you?

To summarize, growing a believer in maturity isn't a precocial approach; we shouldn't trust an individual to launch successfully without much outside guidance. But it isn't an altricial approach either, which assumes that new faith requires a long incubation and low expectations. So how do we develop believers into the type of maturity Paul prays for in Philippians 1? The answer is best seen in Jesus (and in the Peregrine Falcon).

The Maker's Dozen

Although Jesus certainly covered a lot of ground and influenced many people in three years of ministry, I regularly forget this shocking fact: His nest only contained twelve eggs.

By today's standards of leadership development strategy, that seems shortsighted, doesn't it? Don't you expect more from your pastor, or even from your parish elder or small group leader? Wouldn't you want to see a bit more pizzazz in your missionary's monthly update? Just twelve eggs? (And, let's be frank, only eleven that hatched.) The Lord of the cosmos, the creator and sustainer of life itself, steps into this world for three years to create a global movement of grace. Think of the possibilities! A series of large-scale leadership conferences, perhaps? A multi-week convention at the Galilee Civic Center? An international speaking tour?

No. A dozen eggs.

Jesus's method was life-on-life. It wasn't life-on-curriculum or life-on-crowd. He invited twelve unlikely men into the patterns of his own life. They got him for far more than a one-hour service on the Sabbath (which, sadly, is as far as a discipleship strategy goes in many churches, expecting a weekly sermon to do all the heavy lifting). They watched him get up early in the morning to pray. They listened to his interactions with groups and individuals, learned from his dinner conversations, and attended weddings and funerals. Along the way, Jesus involved them in his work, sending them out two by two to repeat his message (Matthew 10:1; Mark 6:7).

Jesus did not simply give directives and expect his followers to comply. That's how I'm prone to disciple, if I'm honest. *Let me tell you what to do, and then you go do it.* It's superprecocial; I want my disciples to crack that eggshell and hit the ground with their feet already moving. Instead, Jesus took the long view, knowing that he wasn't just making disciples but making disciple*makers*—an exponential investment at a patient pace.

A discipling pace provides the necessary time for the life of faith to be absorbed at a deeper level. It might start with directing (I do, you watch), but it doesn't end there. Gradually, it will include plenty of equipping (I do, you help) and supporting (you do, I help), until finally we settle into the role of empowering (you do, I watch). This requires a whole lot of life-on-life patience, with mentor and apprentice walking the same dusty roads together. It would be a stretch to call Jesus's method efficient by modern standards, but it proved to be *effective,* right?

Five years ago, my church decided that the future of our discipleship strategy would consist of slow, intentional investment in a select few, who would then do the same in others.[7] Start small and go deep. But to be honest, for results-oriented Americans like us, starting small is tough. After all, a cornerstone ministry needs a big, shiny launch event, doesn't it? Instead we started with just six people, a ministry so purposefully small that we couldn't even advertise it. At the end of a full year, we had actually managed to *shrink* the ministry to five people. Was anything ever going to hatch from this nest?

Remember, though, our goal wasn't to make disciples but to make disciple*makers*—disciples who had a vision to make disciples. Each of our remaining five committed to strategically disciple three other people for the next three years (just like Jesus). And although this "cornerstone ministry" was barely visible to the wider church, something wonderful was incubating. Group participants were imparted with the necessary tools to be group leaders, as five became twenty, and then twenty became fifty, and we're fully on track to see a hundred and fifty kingdom-minded disciplemakers in the next five years.

It's the tortoise and the hare. Before you go fast, you've got to go slow. Ask the fastest animal on the planet, the Peregrine Falcon. Adult peregrines have been clocked at speeds up to 238 miles per hour in an aerial dive called a "stoop." That's slightly faster than the top speed of a Formula One race car. But teaching a young falcon how to handle that sort of power involves a process of slow discipleship. When the nestlings are around six weeks old, the parents will coax the fledglings to ponder life outside the nest by bringing some fresh prey within sight. This is stage one. Once the young leave the nest, that's where the real life-on-life discipleship begins, as the parents create increasingly challenging maneuvers to train their youngsters in basic aeronautics. They'll work through follow-the-leader games, advance to holding prey in midair, practice mid-flight food transfer, and graduate to catching free-falling food. Over a six-month span, falcons learn how to be falcons, built for speed and stooping from new heights.

Falcon discipleship is about more than just leaving the nest; it's about becoming equipped for the roles they were made for. By God's grace, that's what my church is learning to do, as we embrace the long-term, life-on-life approach of Jesus. Our leaders model the journey of faith, coach in spiritual growth goals, exemplify a life of repentance, serve the community alongside their groups, and transparently live out the Great Commission.

Do you see how important this equipping is? People often

tell me that they've left a church (either another for ours or ours for another) because "I just wasn't being fed there." Granted, a good church will feed you. But a *faithful* church will teach you, like the peregrine, how to feed yourself.

I don't know the ideal time for a child to leave the parental nest. But spiritually speaking, the goal is ever-increasing maturity on the journey from the little white egg to the great white throne. You were made to grow as a disciple who "abound[s] more and more in knowledge and depth of insight." Even more than that, you were made to transfer these things into the lives of others, sharing and replicating "the fruit of righteousness that comes through Jesus Christ—to the glory and praise of God" (Philippians 1:9–11).

That's what you were hatched for.

— CHAPTER 4 —

Bird Funerals

For to me, to live is Christ and to die is gain.

—PHILIPPIANS 1:21

Remember there is a future after the sand runs out, and that future is already bleeding into your present. *Dum spiro spero:* while I breathe, I hope.

—JAMES K. A. SMITH[1]

VINCENT HAGEL, A Washington State birder and Audubon chapter president, was visiting a friend when he noticed a commotion outside the kitchen window. In the yard, a crow lay dead, and a dozen other crows had encircled the body, hopping up and down in an agitated gathering. Eventually one of the crows flew off briefly, returning with a small twig in its beak. Approaching the fallen comrade, it laid the twig on the body and flew away. As Hagel watched in amazement, the other eleven birds repeated the gesture, one at a time, each one flying off briefly to return with its own contribution—a twig or blade of grass. Within five minutes, the crows had all flown away, and the dead bird lay alone, covered in the offerings of its fellow birds.[2]

This strange death observance isn't a unique occurrence among the corvids—that highly intelligent family of birds that includes jays, crows, magpies, and ravens. Ravens have been observed assembling around the base of a power transformer where two fellow birds had been electrocuted. Flocks of Black-billed Magpies gather within minutes of a newly-discovered magpie carcass.[3] But perhaps the most extensive effort in understanding "bird funerals" was a 2012 UC Davis study on the Western Scrub-jay (renamed the California Scrub-jay in 2018).[4]

Using fourteen feeder sites throughout Davis, California, the study team created a series of control experiments to try to better understand the behavior of scrub-jays around a dead bird. To start, a dead jay was placed a few feet from an established feeder. The first jay to discover the deceased began a loud chatter that's been termed a *zeep*, a *zeep-scold*, or a *scold*—which essentially sounds like a really angry zipper. Within minutes, a full flock of jays arrived, each bird joining the chatter with plenty of *zeeps* of their own. The researchers referred to this gathering as a "cacophonous aggregation." The scrub-jays didn't just gather for a momentary gawk. The cacophony sometimes lasted half an hour, as the birds circled the body and—to all outward appearances—worked through their grief together.

Scrub-jays reserve this behavior only for funerals. When decoys (bird-shaped blocks of wood complete with popsicle-stick feathers) are placed at the feeders, the birds don't react at all, proving that all those screaming zeeps aren't just an alarm over something odd or novel. A taxidermy mount of a jay doesn't get a rise out of the birds either; it appears alive enough, and thus doesn't garner any sympathy. But place a dead bird on the ground, and the zeeps will flow freely. The birds will even stop eating—sometimes for more than twenty-four hours.

"The jury is still out on whether birds grieve their own," says author Jennifer Ackerman. "But more and more scientists seem willing to admit the possibility."[5] She notes that a Greylag Goose that has lost a mate can show physical symptoms similar to human grief: head-hanging, sullenness, and sunken eyes. The same behaviors are seen in widowed parrots, which may become lethargic or refuse to eat. And other birds with strong pair-bonds, like Bewick's Swans, exhibit mourning behavior for a year or more.

Those bird accounts, in my mind, bear a strange affinity to the typical behaviors I've seen in the many funerals I've officiated as a pastor. Crows bearing twigs strangely resemble the family members who line up to lay roses on a casket, or loved ones who assemble a foyer table of mementos and photos. The "year of mourning" is a human phenomenon too; isn't "zeeping" one of the five stages of grief?

So what does a bird understand about death? From a scientific point of view, of course, we tread with care, cautious not to wrongly overlay the human experience onto these avian observations. Are the scrub-jay zeeps simply a warning call, alerting others to be cautious around this apparent crime scene? Is their fasting a learned behavior to avoid a dangerous area, poisoned food, or the spread of disease? Is this flocking behavior an example of the evolutionary advantages of social cohesion? Scientifically, those explanations make sense. But how do we explain the crow offerings to a fallen bird or the sullen behavior of a bereaved goose or parrot? What adaptive behavior is at work there? Admittedly, it's a mystery, but doesn't it seem likely that these birds comprehend something about death?

When a Cell Becomes a Celebration

So, for mortals of the human variety, how are we to think about that moment in the not-too-distant future when friends and family will (metaphorically, I assume) lay their twig eulogies over our tomb? Paul's letter to the Philippians is a paradigm shaper for us because he writes it on the potential cusp of death. He's no stranger to near-death experiences, having survived at least five severe lashings, three beatings with rods, and three shipwrecks. (Personally, if I were Paul, after the first shipwreck—or definitely after the second one—I would opt for land routes.) There was also a stoning, a venomous snakebite, and "a night and a day in the open sea" (2 Corinthians 11:24–25). Ponder that list of harrowing escapes for a moment. Any one of those incidents is a terrifying action-movie sequence; imagine yourself treading water on the heaving waves of a Mediterranean storm or dodging the rocks of an angry mob. A near-death experience gives you a more clearheaded perspective on life, and Paul has had more than a dozen. He has a martyr's résumé. I want to learn about how to face death from a guy like *that.*

Paul's current imprisonment in Rome could easily end in execution. Spoiler alert: It doesn't. Paul will be released after two years in Rome, then go on to minister for another six or seven years before another Roman imprisonment finally ends his run, earthly speaking (2 Timothy 4:6–8). This current incarceration will end in his release, and Paul seems to sense it:

"For I know that through your prayers and God's provision of the Spirit of Jesus Christ what has happened to me will turn out for my deliverance" (Philippians 1:19). Soon he'll be back in action, reactivated as a map-trotting missionary, singing the song of a freed bird as Roman cell doors swing wide:

> Praise be to the LORD,
> who has not let us be torn by their teeth.
> We have escaped like a bird
> from the fowler's snare;
> the snare has been broken,
> and we have escaped. (Psalm 124:6–7)

Parole notwithstanding, Paul is ready for anything. Life and death lay before him like the two options in a choose-your-own-adventure book. He'll take whatever the Lord gives, "For to me, to live is Christ and to die is gain" (Philippians 1:21).

Some have called this Paul's finest moment, the attitudes of the gospel laid out in just seven Greek words. But as inspiring as those seven words sound, many of us find it terrifying to stare death in the face with that sort of joy. As a pastor, I've seen many believers die with undaunted hope. I've also seen believers come unglued in fear and disbelief. Granted, if our faith is genuine, a mustard seed of it is enough, so in the end, it's not about the amount of our confidence but *whom* our confidence is in. But personally, I want my last earthly moments to be defined by bold, unflinching assurance, don't you?

To Die Is Gain

"To die is gain" isn't just positive thinking or a nice spin on a sad moment. It's the conviction that one day (to quote my favorite authors, Lewis and Tolkien, in one half sentence) death itself will work backward[6] and everything sad will come untrue.[7] It's the conviction that in conquering my sin, Jesus Christ has also conquered the *wages* of my sin, death itself (Romans 6:23). For those who by faith are united to Jesus, *his* resurrection promises the certainty of our own: "Christ has indeed been raised from the dead, the firstfruits of those who have fallen asleep" (1 Corinthians 15:20).

One of my favorite descriptions of our future hope comes from the Puritan Richard Baxter. He suffered from a very frail constitution and, faced with his own likely death in 1647 at the age of thirty-one, began writing down the reflections he hoped might be shared at his funeral. He surprised himself and others by surviving the illness and living another forty-five years, but his premature parting words became the beloved book, *The Saint's Everlasting Rest.* Baxter wrote,

> When we have reached the harbor, we have finished sailing.... Thus there will be no more prayer, because there will be no more necessity, only the full enjoyment of what we prayed for. We will not need to fast, weep, and watch anymore, being out of the reach of sin and temptations. Nor will we need instruction and exhortation: preaching is done; ministry ceases; the sacraments are now past their use....
>
> Doubtless, there is no such thing as grief and sorrow there. Nor is there such a thing as a pale face, feeble joints, languishing sickness, groaning fears, consuming cares, or whatever deserves the name of evil. A gale of groans and a stream of tears will accompany us to the very gates, and there they will bid us farewell forever. Our sorrow will be turned into joy, and no one will take our joy from us.[8]

With those prizes before us, how can a believer help but see death as an exponential gain? That future hope changes our present realities, making us long for the day when all things are made new.

One of my seminary professors was a man named Jack Arnold, a plucky preacher who also served as my wife's pastor before I met her. On January 9, 2005, Jack was preaching at his church in Orlando about this very passage from Philippians, describing verse 21 as his favorite verse in Scripture. With the enthusiasm born of decades of faithful service, he said these words: "To live is Christ and to die is . . . terrible? awful? tragedy? No! To live is *Christ* and to die is *gain*! I am ready to go and be with the Lord. Until my work on this earth is done, I am immortal. But *when* my work for Christ is done . . ." At this moment he slapped his hands together toward the sky and exclaimed, "I am outta here! I don't know about you, but when my work is done, I go to be with Jesus. And that will be *gain.* And when I go to heaven . . ." He halted on those words, looked up for a moment and swayed, grabbed the pulpit, and fell to the floor, immediately dead of a heart attack. Immediately home. Immediately before the face of God.

That, my friends, is how to preach this passage. Like I said, I long for my last breath to be a sigh of victory.

Admittedly, you only get to preach that sermon once.

Death-Redefining Birds

For many people across the centuries, resurrection has been a thing with feathers. As early as the late first century, Christian theologians like Clement, Tertullian, Ambrose, Jerome, Origen, and Cyril of Jerusalem compared resurrection hope to a bird that you'll never see in your field guide—the phoenix. This mythological creature was said to die in flames every five hundred years, only to rise from the ashes to new life. Early church fathers borrowed from this ancient Greek/

Egyptian story to illustrate the concept of death giving way to new life.[9]

It wasn't the best example, honestly, and these writers could be accused of either cultural syncretism or biological gullibility. (Clement, for instance, wrote with the assumption that the bird actually existed.) The phoenix's ageless cycle of death and rebirth is probably better suited to reincarnation than resurrection, since ultimately the Christian hope is not cyclical but linear—a timeline with a past and a future. Nonetheless, for many in the early church, the phoenix was a fitting image of Christ's resurrection, which is why you'll still find the phoenix in the occasional cathedral mosaic or fresco.

Perhaps there's a better bird to embody our resurrection hope, though it's far less majestic, and, well, you might not like it.

What about a vulture?

It's true that we use this word as an epithet against sleazy lawyers and predatory lenders. It's also an apt descriptor of Marvel villains, lurking internet trolls, and children who snatch the best offerings at church potlucks. No one wants to be called a vulture.

I doubt anyone associates the word *hope* with a vulture. Courtney Ellis writes, "In trees they sit hunched, looking a little put off. They are the librarian when your book is overdue, the doctor when you won't take your medication. They're not mad; they're just disappointed."[10] If I see vultures circling me overhead on a hike, I get nervous, wondering if they know something I don't know about the difficulty of this trail—maybe placing bets on my fitness odds.

What does the beauty of God's resurrection have in common with such a subjectively disgusting bird? I mean, a Turkey Vulture projectile vomits when threatened. That's a gross reflex under any conditions, but especially considering what sort of meal it's projecting. It defecates on its feet to cool down. It sports a head free of feathers so that it won't get roadkill parts stuck in its coiffure. It hunches unglamorously, with a head too small for its body and nostrils you can see through to the other side. Its only sound is a high-pitched hiss.

Yes, vultures are gross, but also grossly misunderstood, and a world *without* vultures would be far more disgusting. Vultures are nature's janitors, quietly and efficiently removing the world of its unsightly trash. Without them, death would literally "pile up" on us, an unsanitary mess of slowly rotting decay. As much as we associate vultures with death, they don't actually kill anything. While more conventionally "noble" birds like eagles shred their screaming prey apart, vultures by contrast *remove* the remains of death and violence. Their digestive juices are superpowered, remarkable at purifying and neutralizing even anthrax, rabies, and other death-sentence pathogens. The vulture removes the toxicity of death. The Mayans called them "death eaters."

Author Debbie Blue writes, "Vultures stare death in the face and fear it not at all. It goes through their bodies and comes out harmless. They cleanse the world."[11] With that reality in mind, the Turkey Vulture's scientific name is surprisingly beautiful. It is *Cathartes aura*—translated either as "purifying breeze" or "golden purifier." Its genus name is the source of our word *catharsis.*

All analogies break down if you take them too far, and let's agree that there are plenty of ways in which Jesus is *not at all* like a Turkey Vulture. But for starters, we remember that "He had no beauty or majesty to attract us to him, nothing in his appearance that we should desire him" (Isaiah 53:2). His plumage wasn't eye-catching. More importantly, we're reminded of the Bible's taunt to death itself, "'Where, O death, is your victory? Where, O death, is your sting?' The sting of death is sin, and the power of sin is the law. But thanks be to God! He gives us the victory through our Lord Jesus Christ" (1 Corinthians 15:55–57).

Jesus came into this world to defang death. Death is *not* a natural part of living, *que será será,* the circle of life. The Bible portrays it as the enemy. But in Christ it is a defeated enemy! You can't write that without exclamation points. Jesus is the conquering Savior who makes even death nontoxic, choking it down on the cross and rendering it innocuous by his resurrection: "Death has been swallowed up in victory" (1 Corinthians 15:54). Jesus is our Golden Purifier, and those who trust in him by faith need not fear death.

Paul wrote to the Philippians that "it is more necessary for you that I remain" (1:24). But Jesus's job description was this: "It is more necessary for you that I die." Jesus set aside comfort, glory, and reputation to be humiliated on a cross, effectively saying, "I will forgo what's good for me to do what's best for you. My death is your gain." The reason that death is gain for the believer is that Jesus didn't pursue what was best for *him;* instead he willingly sacrificed for what was best for *us.* He won by losing. He conquered death by dying. When we live in that resurrection reality, with the promise of life before us in both this life and the next, then we're ready, like Paul, to go or to stay. To live is Christ; to die is gain.

To quote Keats, "Thou wast not born for death, immortal Bird!"[12] The church, the body of Christ, is united to a living and resurrected Savior, and because he lives, we too shall live. His resurrection previews our own, taking the venom from death's fangs. Those words from Psalm 124, so appropriate to Paul's prison break, are our words as well: "We have escaped like a bird from the fowler's snare."

"Until my work on this earth is done, I am immortal. But when my work for Christ is done . . . I am outta here! When my work is done, I go to be with Jesus. And that will be gain. And when I go to heaven . . ."

— CHAPTER 5 —

Birdnados & Murmurations

Therefore if you have any encouragement from being united with Christ, if any comfort from his love, if any common sharing in the Spirit, if any tenderness and compassion, then make my joy complete by being like-minded, having the same love, being one in spirit and of one mind.

—PHILIPPIANS 2:1–2

Blest be the tie that binds
our hearts in Christian love;
the fellowship of kindred minds
is like to that above.

—JOHN FAWCETT[1]

IF YOU'VE EVER observed a tight-knit flock of birds racing overhead and asked yourself, "How do they do that?" or "How come they don't hit each other?" or "Which one's in charge anyway?" you're not alone in your questions. In fact, the formations of flocking birds have garnered the interest of physicists, psychologists, hedge-fund managers, nanobot developers, mathematicians, civil engineers, movie CGI teams, and even concert crowd-control planners. In recent years, all these fields have attempted to unlock one of nature's great secrets: How do birds coordinate themselves into a united, tightly choreographed unit?

Maybe theologians ask the same question. After all, could the forces that hold a flock together also be a living metaphor for the unseen forces that hold God's church together? At the end of Philippians 1 and the beginning of Philippians 2, Paul describes two beautiful realities: union with Christ and unity among believers. Simply put, we are meaningfully connected to the Savior, and because of that, we're also meaningfully connected to the saved—something we confess in the Apostles' Creed when we speak of "the communion of saints." That invisible connection is tough for us to get our heads wrapped around, but when I try to picture the phenomenon, two bird species come to mind—both frankly unflattering in isolation, but poetic in greater numbers.

Birdnado

The Chimney Swift isn't much to look at—basically a cigar strapped to a boomerang. Its dull-brown body is vaguely tapered at both ends: a short stiff tail at one end and a short stiff beak at the other, so those arced boomerang wings are really the only thing telling you if it's coming or going. Due to their stiff wingbeats and high-pitched twittering, along with the fact that they love to roost in chimneys, they're often mistaken for bats. If I were a bird, I'd probably be offended by that.

They do have offsetting assets; most notably, swifts were built to fly, and fly fast (after all, *swift* would be a terrible name for a slow bird). The Vaux's Swift in the Western United States can top out at around two hundred miles per hour, almost keeping pace with a diving Peregrine Falcon. For all their speed, though, they lack maneuverability; their short wing bones don't have the joint flexibility of most birds. This means they're not great at takeoffs and landings, and when you couple that with feet ill-equipped for perching, it's no surprise that a swift spends about ten months of the year airborne.

So behold: a drab-colored, blunt-bodied, stiff-winged, perch-impeded creature. I have not painted a complimentary picture. But given sufficient numbers, this bird will take your breath away. It happens here in North Carolina, where I live, for one week every fall, and each year I enjoy loading the family into the minivan at dusk to drive to one of the old high schools in our area—the ones old enough to have a furnace with a brick chimney. A normally bustling school looks deserted at dusk, but just open the car doors and look up, and suddenly you're standing in the eye of the perfect storm.

I remember our first encounter. The five of us watched pre-dusk as thousands of Chimney Swifts flapped in a chaotic cloud above us, their batlike twitter filling the air. As dusk approached, the dark cloud slowly formed into a clockwise arc as more and more birds joined the invisible circular track. Within minutes, thousands of birds had created what my kids perfectly described as a "birdnado." We stood in the eye of a revolving mass of birds, a thick funnel in tight formation pointing like a finger at the school chimney. I counted them as they dropped in groups into the stack: 450 . . . 500 . . . 1,000 . . . 2,000 . . . still going, straining the chimney's capacity like clowns packing into a circus car. Since swifts lack wing agility, entering the chimney means approaching it at full speed and then stalling out directly over it, falling in and presumably grabbing hold of something on the way down. I counted very conservatively as 2,500 birds dropped into that single structure. Another birder had visited the spot three days prior and counted 8,000.

By the time the last bird had flopped into the stack, the sky had gone dark and silent. My kids became avid swift fans of the non-Taylor variety that night.

Aerial Jazz

At least with Chimney Swifts there are survival-related explanations for their gymnastics. Their chimney roost is a necessary rest-and-refuel stop on the way to their wintering grounds in South America. But the purposes of a pulsing flock of European Starlings are much less obvious. If swift art could be considered utilitarian, a starling murmuration is the extravagance of art for art's sake.

Like the swift, the starling isn't much to look at, although it's a noticeable upgrade. Birders don't tend to fawn over a starling, and many people (especially farmers) consider them a nuisance. At a glance, a starling is a short-tailed black bird with a seasonally-yellow beak—not anything to turn your binoculars. My kids' generation would dismiss them with the word *basic.* In the right light, however, they possess a surprising beauty, an iridescence that reflects deep purples and greens from their shaggy feathers.

Their coloration is fleeting and subtle, but starlings have a grander beauty that, when displayed, is impossible to miss. In large groups—generally from late fall through the end of winter, and usually near dusk—a flock performs a show so unique it deserves its own word: *murmuration.* The term is an attempt to capture the sound, the wingbeats of thousands of birds thrumming in unison, something that Annie Dillard described as "a sound of beaten air, like a million shook rugs, a muffled whuff."[2] Perhaps a word can capture this stunning sound, but no word can capture the sight. It is a living curtain of feathers, a dark, elegant wave, an aerial Rorschach inkblot. John Updike called it "a great scarf of birds,"[3] and Richard Wilbur said that "they roll like a drunken fingerprint across the sky."[4] A murmuration is the finest improv jazz. It's a dance.

A starling murmuration may include up to *five million birds,* and when it self-assembles, it gives the appearance of a collective mind. The flock hovers over a field in tight formation with graceful, almost instantaneous changes of direction. Both the how and the why of a murmuration continue to baffle scientists, who have broken the flock down to the smallest units to better understand the rules under which each bird operates. Though it may appear that a collective consciousness is at work, our best current understanding is that these birds are simply following the cues of the six or seven immediate neighbors around, above, and below them. The rules are basic enough: stay together, match velocity, avoid collisions. But to play by these rules, starlings need to think fast; studies have clocked their reaction time at fifteen milliseconds—ten times faster than that of a seasoned NASCAR driver.

The Golden Thread

In these two examples, the flock makes the ordinary extraordinary. Swifts and starlings, run-of-the-mill creatures in isolation, find their beauty by coming together. Perhaps the swifts' funnel cloud and the starlings' pulsing sky jazz are lessons in the nature of the church's unity as Paul describes it in Philippians 1:27:

> Whatever happens, conduct yourselves in a manner worthy of the gospel of Christ. Then, whether I come and see you or only hear about you in my absence, I will know that you stand firm in the one Spirit, striving together as one for the faith of the gospel.

For Paul, the picture of a healthy church community was one of unity. A few verses later he throws down the gauntlet to the Philippians: If the gospel means anything to you at all, "make my joy complete by being like-minded, having the same love, being one in spirit and of one mind" (Philippians 2:2). The evidence of a changed individual is seen in a changed community. Grace reshapes the way we connect. What does it look like to live like the gospel is worthy? Live *unified.* In fact, live who you already *are.* Let me explain.

Picture your Sunday morning gathering for a moment. Perhaps you attend a glitzy church full of impressively glamorous people. But it's far more likely the saints assembled in your church possess a swift-and-starling commonness: a congregated cross section of average Joes and plain Janes, or what C. S. Lewis's Screwtape referred to as "neighbours [who] sing out of tune, or have boots that squeak, or double chins, or odd clothes."[5] As you look around the room, you are beholding what theologians have historically called the *visible church*—the church as observed by the naked human eye, a gathering of those who profess belief. Whether or not they *possess* what they *profess,* only God knows. We can't accurately perceive another person's heart, but what we *do* know is that Jesus himself differentiated true faith from mere verbal profession (Matthew 7:22–23).

So here's the challenge for us. The visible church is the church as we *experience* it, but it's not the full picture of what the church truly *is*. We might be tempted to look around on a Sunday morning and feel (to be frank) under-impressed. Even the hippest churches with the trendiest music and the tastiest fair-trade coffee still bear little resemblance to a heavenly army arrayed in all its splendor. Amid all those squeaky boots and double chins, where's this so-called power that the gates of hell can't stand against?

But now let me ask you to stretch your imagination to picture that same Sunday gathering from the perspective of heaven. With the veil lifted, you would realize that you sit among immortals, cohesively unified (even when they don't act like it) because Christ the King is the head that holds every cell of the body together (1 Corinthians 12:18–20; Colossians 1:18). A bond unites you to them, and them to each other. For the sake of your imagination, picture that bond as a thin golden thread. It's not a thread of your own making but a picture of what Jesus is making *us*, and it means that if you're united to Christ, you are by definition (whether you like it or not) united to these other true believers around you, in the most real of ways, as you sing songs and break bread and drink that fair-trade coffee in the foyer. The threads interlace the room—the "blessed tie" we sing about that "binds our hearts in Christian love."

But don't stop there. Now picture that golden thread continuing out the sanctuary door, down streets and sidewalks, to knit with other believers in your community—many of them gathering in their own church sanctuaries, others worshipping in isolation at home, still others serving their community in works of necessity and mercy.

Keep going. The thread spans borders and oceans to cast a net over hope-filled believers everywhere, connecting you to ordinary saints of different languages, cultures, and settings, unified by the same Christ.

And as if that's not beautiful enough, don't forget the fourth dimension; the thread also weaves backward in time, connecting the saints of today with those who have gone before us. It weaves forward as well, through new generations yet unborn, to the final destination when the whole connected gathering is fully assembled.

Every believer in that golden-threaded web (if I may now change the metaphor) is circling the chimney of that great white throne, until the moment our Savior beckons us into his rest.

Your Sunday morning gathering of everyday people may seem ordinary in isolation, but the invisible realities that hold it together are astounding. This is the invisible church. Listen carefully and you may hear the murmuring wingbeats of the saints.

The Flock of God

The Bible uses multiple metaphors to depict this invisible-church reality, and no one picture does justice to the relationship. We are the body of which Christ is the head. We are the bride of which Christ is our bridegroom. We are the branches of which Christ is the vine. But it occurs to me that there is another image used throughout Scripture that we often forget. We are the *flock* of God.

Granted, the Bible is generally referring to a flock of *sheep.* I get it. But the description of the people of God as a group of animals, whether feathered or fuzzy, helps us understand what God is up to. Jesus describes his flock with tenderness (Luke 12:32) and purposefulness (John 10:16). And when Paul and Peter exhort church leaders in their role, they invoke the same flock language (Acts 20:28–29; 1 Peter 5:2).

Imagine the witness of the church to the world if we behaved by the starlings' set of rules: stay together, match velocity, avoid collisions. Can we embody the benefits of staying in tight formation while doing everything we can to avoid knocking each other down? The church has not always done this well. Especially in recent years, the flock has witnessed plenty of collisions. It's been suggested by some researchers that in a murmuration, we may be witnessing a group movement in which each individual bird is essentially casting a vote—a delegation of bird citizenry in the process of seeking a final consensus. Seeking consensus is rarely that beautiful. If the American church were a murmuration, that aerial inkblot might have fractured into several mini-flocks by now, with plenty of collateral damage strewn on the ground. This doesn't change the reality that the invisible church is God's flock: The golden thread persists despite our failures to live up to it. Joni Eareckson Tada writes, "Believers are never told to *become* one; we already *are* one and are expected to act like it."[6] Sheep bite, birds collide, and yet the Good Shepherd faithfully holds his flock together, calling us to something better. I'm convicted, as a pastor, that a shepherd has no leg to stand on when he complains about his flock. What did I expect? Does a surgeon complain that "there's too much blood around this place"? No, it's the job. It's why we're there. I long to be a more cooperative, patient, and gracious wingmate.

So how *do* we "act like it"? I've tried recently to see my faith experiences with murmuration in mind—to be mindful of the oneness of God's flock, listening for the rhythm of the saints. As I do, the golden thread manifests itself more tangibly, in two ways.

First, through my newsfeed, I witness secondhand the heartbreak of suffering. Paul writes about the body of Christ, "If one part suffers, every part suffers with it; if one part is honored, every part rejoices with it" (1 Corinthians 12:26). Scenes of war in distant lands feature believers singing hymns in darkened buildings, claiming God's promises amid the rumble of tanks, bombs, and gunfire. Pastors gather to dispense mercy and put themselves in harm's way. In other corners of the world, believers pick up the pieces of burned-out churches, targeted for the God they worship. Others cling to God's promises in political prisons for trumped-up crimes stemming from their ardent faith.

The body of Christ is a flock circling the same chimney, headed for the same home, a cloud of witnesses. When one part hurts, we all feel the wound. It sends us to our knees in prayer and mobilizes us to help where we can. Even as I write this, I have a pit in my stomach as I reflect on the suffering of the saints around the world.

Second, the golden thread has transformed my experience of Sunday worship. I've started listening more intently to the voices around me as I sing, feeling the melody of our common faith. I feel it especially around the Lord's Supper, when we remind ourselves of Christ's work on our behalf. As is customary in my own congregation, we take the bread individually to remember the personal work of Jesus to redeem our hearts, but we take the cup together to remember the communal work of Jesus in rescuing his church. In those brief moments, I am newly aware that the Table is not just about *me* and Jesus but *we* and Jesus. I hear the first-person plural in our closing song, rejoicing not only that Jesus has died for me but that he has died for the people *around* me—people I love deeply. I listen for the thrumming wingbeats of the saints, flying in formation.

"Do not be afraid, little flock, for your Father has been pleased to give you the kingdom" (Luke 12:32).

The flock of God is a murmuration, dancing in the sky like grace.

— CHAPTER 6 —

Treecreeper Humility

Have the same mindset as Christ Jesus:

> Who, being in very nature God,
> did not consider equality with God something
> to be used to his own advantage;
> rather, he made himself nothing
> by taking the very nature of a servant.
>
> —PHILIPPIANS 2:5–7

The bird that soars on highest wing,
Builds on the ground her lowly nest;
And she that doth most sweetly sing,
Sings in the shade when all things rest:
—In lark and nightingale we see
What honour hath humility.

—JAMES MONTGOMERY[1]

SO, WHICH BIRD is the biggest jerk?

That was the exact question posited in a recent *Washington Post* article, summarizing an elaborate study on pecking order at the bird feeder.[2] By using observations from over thirty thousand bird-feeder-watching citizens like you and me and recording almost one hundred thousand interactions, researchers created an impressive "power rankings" list of bird aggression among species at bird feeders across North America. In a face-off between any two birds, who will flinch first? The study predicts interactions among two hundred species, anticipating who will assert dominance and who will chicken out.

The birds at the top of the list likely wouldn't surprise you. Once you remove the unlikely oddities (personally, I've never had a Gambel's Quail or a Black-bellied Whistling Duck at my feeder), the reigning king of the backyard is the American Crow, to whom all but a turkey or raven will readily acquiesce. An assortment of woodpeckers also made the top fifteen, along with the ever-confident Northern Mockingbird and the ever-irritating Common Grackle. And if a flock of Blue Jays has ever reminded you of an unpleasant playground run-in with school bullies, now you have scientific evidence to support your assessment.

But as I scanned this assemblage of avian antagonists, I found myself asking, "So who's at the *bottom*?" What does the *opposite* of aggression look like? Scanning to the bottom of the top two hundred—beneath the bunting, junior to the junco, lesser than a Lesser Goldfinch—sits the North American humility champion of the bird world: the Brown Creeper.

The Brown Creeper is a tiny woodland bird that's reminiscent of a wind-up toy. Its two short feet stay together as it hops rapidly, its head bobbing forward slightly with each quick motion. Now imagine that mechanical cadence of *hop-bob-hop-bob* scooting rapidly up the trunk of a tree in a spiral pathway. The creeper stops long enough to pry an insect out of the bark, but it doesn't rest for long. Like a wind-up toy, it doesn't like to stop once it's started.

All nine species of treecreepers (most of them Eurasian) are common and yet rare to see, at least in my experience. They're patterned in various shades of mottled drab brown, effectively camouflaging them against a tree-bark background. The naturalist W. M. Tyler described the bird as "a fragment of detached bark that is defying the law of gravitation by moving upward over the trunk."[3]

But the most unique aspect of a treecreeper's movement, and what makes its identification unmistakable, is not how it behaves on a tree but what it does *between* trees. When the treecreeper reaches the top of its pathway, it dives hastily downward to the base of a new tree, "resembl[ing] a little dry leaf blown about by the wind."[4] Never outward or upward, always downward. The pathway it travels through the forest is that of a swing-set slide: a steep ladder ascent and then a swooping downhill glide back to level ground again.

In other words, the treecreeper always starts low. When it ascends, it does so only to descend again. After taking all the trouble to work its way up a tree, it could presumably hop through the upper canopy and enjoy the efforts of its arduous climb. Instead, it chooses to approach every tree from the bottom. The way to the next tree is from the ground. The way up is down.

Down Is the New Up

The virtue of humility operates in the same way.

Paul tells the Philippians, "Do nothing out of selfish ambition or vain conceit. Rather, in humility value others above yourselves, not looking to your own interests but each of you to the interests of the others" (Philippians 2:3–4). Easier said than done. Pride hides well from our skewed self-assessments. C. S. Lewis called it "the great sin" for this reason, stating, "There is no fault which makes a man more unpopular, and no fault which we are more unconscious of in ourselves."[5] Pride is unbelievably sneaky. William Farley writes, "Here is the great paradox: the proud man thinks he is humble, but the humble man thinks he is proud."[6] We need guides, coaches, and humble models as we battle our own pride, ambition, and over-assertiveness. Well, wouldn't a bird that ranks two hundredth out of two hundred on the bird-obnoxiousness scale have something to offer us in this regard?

Of course, not all downward paths are humble. For one, humility is not simply thinking less of ourselves or drumming up a sort of groveling attitude. As C. S. Lewis famously said, a truly humble person "will not be thinking about humility: he will not be thinking about himself at all."[7] The goal of humility is not self-loathing or a lack of self-esteem.

Humility also isn't about pretending to be less capable than we actually are. The A+ student who deflects every compliment with the assertion that they're really not that smart is practicing false modesty, not humility.

Nor is humility cowardice—choosing to hide when a courageous voice is needed. Timidity is not a virtue. Even the creeper has been seen at times joining in with the kinglets and nuthatches in mobbing those unrighteous Blue Jays. Sometimes we gotta speak up.

So, what is humility? Picturing the treecreeper on a tree, think of it as the pattern of going low. Or picturing him at the feeder, think of it as the deference of letting the needs of another precede our own, to "value others above yourselves, not looking to your own interests but each of you to the interests of the others" (Philippians 2:3–4). When I imagine the conversation at the bird feeder, the treecreeper says to the other birds, "No, please, friend, you go first; I insist" or "Take my perch, ole chap; I don't mind." Of course, I realize he's not that consciously benevolent, but then again, birds can't talk, so let's just go with it.

You don't need a Bible verse to know humility is a good idea. Generally, the world admires humility and tends to cringe at any whiff of arrogance. But ancient cultures embraced the exact opposite. The Romans, for instance, taught the importance of humility before the gods or before the emperor, but never among equals. In the day-to-day interactions of life, self-promotion was expected, and to be humble was a faux pas. The Greeks extolled the Delphic Canon as the greatest summary of the virtuous life, yet in the 147 qualities described, nothing remotely resembling humility makes the cut. If you read the greats of Greek and Roman history, they assuredly let you know just how great they were. Caesar Augustus pre-wrote his own obituary, painstakingly highlighting his achievements: battles won, buildings constructed, improvements made, even the details of his charitable giving. It reads like an overbearing LinkedIn profile. Prior to the first century A.D., egotism was conventional behavior; it was totally acceptable to "crow" about yourself.

All this is documented in John Dickson's excellent leadership book *Humilitas,* where he poses the questions: When did it become socially acceptable to lower yourself before an equal? When did humility shift from a liability to an asset?[8] According to Dickson, the cultural change happened rather suddenly, sweeping the ancient world like a revolution. The origin of the shift traces back to the middle of the first century, rooted in some teachings about a carpenter from Nazareth in Israel who showed his greatness through humility—and called others to emulate his example.

But what sparked the humility revolution wasn't just the

humble way Jesus *lived;* it was the humble way he *died.* Through Roman eyes, greatness meant pursuing honor and avoiding shame, so Jesus's death either proved him a failure or radically redefined what it means to be great. Indeed, Jesus introduced the world to an upside-down greatness—one defined by humility. If the virtue of humility seems commonplace today, bear in mind that in Jesus's day, it was absolutely countercultural. When Paul taught that our attitude should be the same as that of Christ Jesus (Philippians 2:5), arrogance lost its luster. Down was the new up.

Seven Stages Down

We are far more inspired by the thought that those who hope in the Lord will "soar on wings like eagles" (Isaiah 40:31) than that they will skulk about on tree trunks like creepers. The treecreeper image doesn't have quite the same strength-renewing vision, does it? And yet, we can't forget that the victorious image of soaring eagles came through the humble downward direction of a cross. In Philippians 2:6–11, Paul is likely quoting an early hymn of the new church, which explains why our English translations indent these verses in poetic style. The early church sang the song of their Savior's every-knee-bowed exaltation, but prefaced it with the melody of a sevenfold subjection. It's perhaps the earliest anthem of the humility revolution.

> Who, being in very nature God,
> did not consider equality with God something to be used to his own advantage;
> rather, he made himself nothing
> by taking the very nature of a servant,
> being made in human likeness.

And being found in appearance as a man,
he humbled himself
by becoming obedient to death—
even death on a cross! (Philippians 2:6–8)

Picture for a moment our friend the treecreeper, perched somewhere at the top of a tree trunk, now letting go to plummet farther and farther down, descending one branch at a time through seven stages on his way to the ground. This is the downward flight of our Savior:

1. It starts in verse 6 with a towering description of Jesus: "Who, being in very nature God..." Jesus is unapologetically presented here as fully divine, the second person of the eternal Trinity, in perfect communion with the Father, possessing everything that is essential to being God. This is where the journey starts, but it's where Jesus has eternally been all along, rightfully at the top of the tree.
2. This preeminent one makes a decision not to keep the position of cosmic authority, for he "did not consider equality with God something to be used to his own advantage." Instead, he uses his place of preeminence not to be served but to serve. The One who has every right to say to every molecule of this universe, "Mine!" instead says, "This is my body given for *you*" (Luke 22:19).
3. He continues his descent in verse 7: "Rather, he made himself nothing by taking the very nature of a servant." He sets aside his glory, a steep drop from master of the universe to "May I take your order?" The cosmos gets turned on its head, and the humility revolution begins.
4. But even then, we can imagine other options. Jesus could have come as an *angelic* servant; after all, the angels that serve God are pretty impressive, with all those flaming swords and *fear nots* and trumpets and whatnot. Instead,

though, Jesus jumps down another branch, "being made in human likeness." Rather than a glowing, winged seraphim servant, Jesus comes into the world in the same undignified way that each one of us arrived. To redeem us, he must *become* us, must be our "second Adam" (Romans 5:12–19).

5. He takes another step downward in verse 8: "And being found in appearance as a man." Again, Jesus has options. He could be "made in human likeness" while holding on to privilege—maybe a royal king or noble general or CEO or celebrity influencer. Instead, Jesus comes as a *below*-average Joe. He is born in the worst of conditions, in the back lot with the animals, into a scandalous family situation. If Jesus were born today, it wouldn't be in a gated community or lakefront condo but more likely in some under-resourced corner of the city—on a side street I'd probably avoid after dark. As Philip Yancey wrote, "It seems that God arranged the most humiliating circumstances possible for his entrance, as if to avoid any charge of favoritism."[9]
6. And now we approach the bottom of the tree: "He humbled himself by becoming obedient to death." Don't miss the clear message of the gospel accounts: The One who is fully in control embraces betrayal, arrest, and crucifixion of his own accord (John 10:18). He places himself without defense before the kangaroo courts of Herod and Pilate. He stands intentionally silent before his accusers, showing otherworldly restraint, even with legions of angels dutifully ready at his command. He is painfully obedient to his mission.
7. And at the rock bottom of the downward flight of humility, we read these appalling words: "Even death on a cross!" Jesus willingly steps into the most humiliating,

> shameful, and brutal execution imaginable. Two thousand years of history have sanitized the shock for us: Today the cross is jewelry, a tattoo, no big deal. But if you came to church this Sunday and they had a guillotine on the stage, I'm guessing it would have your full attention for the rest of the service. Jesus enters into a world with crosses in it—and embraces his own.

That's the journey from the top of the tree to the bottom. Jesus moves from God to surrender to servant to human likeness to ordinary humanity to death to cross. This series of acts is the best possible use of the word *condescension*—literally "to descend with." We use that word negatively to refer to those who patronize and talk down to others from their prideful perches. But Jesus *was* superior in every way. His willingness to stoop low, from a stable to a peasant life to a cross, was motivated not by selfish pride but selfless compassion. He was bent on our rescue. He credited his perfect life to us and substituted his perfect death so his people might not die under the weight of their sin. In other words, "God made him who had no sin to be sin for us, so that in him we might become the righteousness of God" (2 Corinthians 5:21).

C. S. Lewis wrote, "In the Christian story God descends to re-ascend. . . . He goes down to come up again and bring the whole ruined world up with Him. One has the picture of a strong man stooping lower and lower to get himself underneath some great complicated burden. He must stoop in order to lift, he must almost disappear under the load before he incredibly straightens his back and marches off with the whole mass swaying on his shoulders."[10]

> Forbid it, Lord, that I should boast
> save in the death of Christ, my God![11]

The way up is down. We soar like eagles because Jesus stooped low like a treecreeper.

Nothing to Crow About

What do we do with that amazing demonstration? If we let it, Jesus's example will motivate our humility and compassion.

A humble self-assessment isn't about groveling or having a wounded self-image; it's about freedom from the treadmill of performance, posturing, and reputation manufacturing. Humility isn't about stooping as low as we can but about standing at our full height—next to the God of the universe. That scale comparison will do all the necessary work in our hearts, reminding us of the cosmic absurdity of pretending the world revolves around us. Everything we have is a gift, from our first breath to our ability to read this sentence. "What do you have that you did not receive? And if you did receive it, why do you boast as though you did not?" (1 Corinthians 4:7). "Thinking humbly" is just another way of saying "thinking rightly."

Once we've properly grounded ourselves to the right elevation, we can go about the business of truly serving others as Jesus did. In the three years that Jesus taught his disciples, he consistently escorted them to the bottom of the tree. He defined greatness as a willingness to "go low" in service to others, saying, "The greatest among you will be your servant" (Matthew 23:11). He warned against clamoring for the seats of honor (Luke 14:7–11), even as James and John awkwardly requested tickets in the front row (Mark 10:35–45). And on the "last night of class" he led his students in a foot-washing exercise meant to model what leadership looks like from the bottom of the trunk (John 13:1–17).

If we maintain a prideful, elevated perch, our acts of service will feel like a pity project—the word *condescension* but with all the negative overtones. But compassion, by definition, is "to suffer *with*." In compassion we come alongside others, shoulder to shoulder, eye to eye, cleansing grungy feet—and we don't need to lower ourselves to do so, because . . . well, we're already there.

So we emulate our Savior's example by putting others first. More than that, we rely on his power to die to self and live for others. We're not naturally good at this, because crow-like haughtiness comes easily to most of us. We would've fit right in about 2,500 years ago, but arrogance hasn't been culturally chic for quite a while, and thanks to the humility revolution, now down is up. Our Lord has turned superiority on its head. Now every morning is another opportunity to drop to the bottom of the tree.

Whatever heights you attain, whatever merits you achieve, start by going low.

— CHAPTER 7 —

Honeyguide Partnerships

Therefore, my dear friends, as you have always obeyed—not only in my presence, but now much more in my absence—continue to work out your salvation with fear and trembling, for it is God who works in you to will and to act in order to fulfill his good purpose.

—PHILIPPIANS 2:12–13

The way of holiness that leads to happiness is a narrow way; there is but just room enough for a holy God and a holy soul to walk together.

—THOMAS BROOKS[1]

IT'S DAWN IN the Niassa National Reserve in Mozambique, and an elder from the Yao tribe steps out of his thatched home, intent on a morning hunt. His goal is to find a beehive and bring back some honey for the family, and he's equipped with a spear and some fire-making equipment to smoke out the bees and nab some honeycomb. But he lacks the most important part—the GPS coordinates of an actual hive. For this, he phones a friend—not with a cell phone or a WhatsApp message, but with a loud noise best described as a *brrrr-humph:* a flamboyantly rolled *R,* followed by an emphatic *humph,* delivered with a question-mark-type ending. A rough English translation might be, "Heyyyyyyy, you there?"

Minutes later, help arrives in the form of a starling-sized pink-beaked bird with white tear-shaped cheek patches. It perches upright on a nearby branch and chatters to the hunter. Then it flies a few trees farther on and stops, twittering. *This way, bud.* The hunter follows. The bird flits forward several trees and perches again, waiting patiently for the hunter to catch up. If the hunter stops, the bird will fly back to re-engage his attention. And so it continues, potentially for the next two hours or more.

The Greater Honeyguide has been true to its name since at least the 1500s, mapping out beehives and helping honey seekers. There are fifteen other honeyguide species too, mostly in Africa, including the Lesser Honeyguide and the Least Honeyguide. They're probably named for their size, not their prowess in the honey-guiding profession, but since only the Greater Honeyguide partners with humans, it feels like a fair ranking.

Imagine, for a moment, the magical feeling of having a wild animal personally escort you through the forest. Sure, this is common fare if you're a Disney princess or a visitor to Narnia, but this is a real-life encounter—a small, excited bird guiding you on an African safari. I once experienced something similar on a canoe trip in Vermont, where a Great Horned Owl flew just ahead of us for four miles down a river, seemingly beckoning us to follow. But in hindsight, I think it was actually trying to get away from us: *Stop following me, you creepy humans!*

The honeyguide and its human eventually come into a clearing, where the bird changes its call or goes completely silent, prompting the hunter's attentiveness to the sound of buzzing in a tall baobab tree. The bird knew where the hive was but couldn't score the honey without risking some painful stings. Now it's got some upgraded tech. The Yao hunter lights a torch, climbs the tree, and smokes out the hive, sedating the bees into a comfortably numb state. That, plus opposable thumbs, makes the hunter a valuable commodity for the bird, who's captivated by the sweet honey, the waxy comb, and especially all those wriggly larvae inside.

The hunter scoops some honeycomb into his basket: mission accomplished. But before he returns home, he'll grab an extra comb and impale it on a nearly branch, payment and a generous tip for his tour guide. The hunter departs, and the bird stays back to enjoy the taste of victory. That parting thank-you gift will keep it well incentivized to respond to the next *brrrr-humph.*

A Joint Venture

No one taught the honeyguide this behavior. Scientists term this practice a "mutualistic interaction," and researcher Claire Spottiswoode from the University of Cambridge says, "It's the only known example of targeted two-way signals between people and a free-living species."[2] Yes, there have been isolated examples of dolphins helping fishermen in Brazil or orcas helping Scottish whalers in Australia, but the honeyguide-human partnership is the most consistent and studied interaction.[3]

Sometimes, as with the Yao, the human initiates the hunt with the *brrrr-humph,* but the Hadza community in Tanzania summons the bird with a whistle, and in Zambia it's drawn by the sound of chopping wood. And often it's not the human but the *bird* who initiates, appearing in the village unprompted with a frenetic chattering that communicates, "Oh man, wait till you see what I just found!"

Mauricio Cantor, a behavioral ecologist at Oregon State University, says, "For humans and animals to join forces like this, a few elements need to be in place." He cites things like the resource abundance and complementary hunting skills. But most importantly, he adds, you have to develop some means of effective communication. "Do we have the same goal? And how are we going to coordinate to do this together?"[4]

Which brings us back to Philippians 2 and a pair of verses that describe the objective of a mind-boggling partnership.

> Therefore, my dear friends, as you have always obeyed—not only in my presence, but now much more in my absence—continue to work out your salvation with fear and trembling, for it is God who works in you to will and to act in order to fulfill his good purpose. (Philippians 2:12–13)

Have you ever thought of your life as one lived in *partnership* with God? It seems almost sacrilegious, imagining a sacred handshake with the Ancient of Days, because—let's be honest—on the surface, we don't offer a lot to the arrangement. God knows where the honey is, and he knows how to get it. He doesn't *need* any information or abilities from us. Any cooperative alliance with the Almighty is ridiculously one-sided, right?

God provides absolutely everything. We're hundred-percent beneficiaries.

And yet these verses suggest a role for us to play—a sort of joint venture with God himself. To use Cantor's description, a partnership means effective communication around a common goal. The Lord calls us to align with *his* goal for our lives, that *his* desire would be *our* desire. And his desire, in these two verses, is our *sanctification*—our ongoing transformation into Christ-likeness. Simply put, God wants you to look like Jesus. He wants your character and actions to increasingly reflect his image. That's the quest that the two of you are setting out on. *You* have a role to play in that (verse 12: "work out your salvation with fear and trembling"), and so does he (verse 13: "for it is God who works in you")—two works that are really one work.

It's easy to get this wrong by giving ourselves either too much credit or too little. If we put all the emphasis on *our* work, we'll assume Jesus did the heavy lifting at the outset, with the cross and the empty tomb, but now the rest is pretty much up to us. He threw us the life preserver—now it's sink or swim. On the flip side, if we put all the emphasis on *God's* work, we'll presume that we can put our faith in neutral and coast to the finish line. Somehow the partnership is about both; God does his thing and we do ours, in tandem—a journey of faith made together.

But what's our role in our spiritual growth, and what's God's? How does this divine partnership play itself out?

Work Out What Was Worked In

Since we know salvation is by grace and not by works, all this talk of "working out our salvation" in verse 12 might make us uncomfortable, along with the ominous call to "fear and trembling." Put it together and we could misunderstand and think Paul's saying, "Let the terror of God's wrath motivate you into getting your act together and earning your own salvation." In war-movie terminology, it's Captain Miller sternly urging Private Ryan in the thick of battle, "Earn this"—remember the horror of this sacrifice we're all making for you now, and let it motivate you to make something of yourself. Don't get me wrong, I love *Saving Private Ryan*. But it's a terrible way to live because at the end of your movie, you'll find yourself standing over a soldier's grave still wondering if you were good enough.

And so, to understand our role in this, let's break it down: first the "fear and trembling" and then the whole business of "work out your salvation." Paul's "fear and trembling" isn't a fear of rejection or condemnation: The perfect love of Christ casts out that kind of fear (Romans 8:1; 1 John 4:18). Rather, coming before God with fear and trembling acknowledges our own vulnerabilities in light of his merciful strength. It's a recognition that we come before a sovereign God humbly, inadequately, and submissively, clinging for dear life to the amazing promises of the gospel through all the challenging trials of life. I love the way Sinclair Ferguson describes it:

> The fear of God . . . is really another way of saying "knowing God." It is a heart-felt love for him because of who he is and what he has done; a sense of being in his majestic presence. It is a thrilling awareness that we have this greatest of all privileges, mingled with a realisation that now the only thing that really matters is his opinion. . . . To fear God is to be sensitive to both his greatness and his graciousness. It is to know him and to love him wholeheartedly and unreservedly.[5]

Think *loving reverence.*

But what does it mean to "work out your salvation"? Clearly

these four words aren't advocating for works righteousness, eroding Paul's teaching everywhere else in the Bible. For example, just a few verses later, he writes about "the righteousness that comes from God on the basis of faith" (Philippians 3:9). We get that. But it's easy to assume our justification (being declared righteous and not guilty) was up to Jesus, while our sanctification (our ongoing walk of faith) is up to us. It feels that way sometimes, if we're honest—like we're trudging into the savanna with a spear and torch, without a honeycomb or honeyguide in sight.

The reality, however, is far greater than our feelings: The same gospel that saves us sanctifies us. The gospel isn't simply the minimum requirement for a heavenly future. For the believer, all of life is the gospel. Tim Keller often said, "The gospel is not just the ABCs but the A to Z of Christianity."[6] It's not just how we become a Christian but how we live and grow and trust and bear fruit and do absolutely *anything* of kingdom good. The whole Christian life, not just the initial just-as-I-am, is lived under the grace of the "easy yoke and light burden" of Jesus (see Matthew 11:30).

So what is our role in this partnership with God? Maybe it's as simple as this: to *cooperate* with his work in us. Or we could think of it as "working out what was worked in"—to "work out" the benefits of what God has already "worked in" by the saving work of Christ. Let's face it; God is *far* more committed to our sanctification than we are. That's verse 13: "It is God who works in you to will and to act in order to fulfill his good purpose." That's *his* role in the partnership. If we have any desire to pursue or obey the Lord ("to will"), he put that there. If we have any capacity to do gospel good in this world ("to act"), he put that there too. Our life in Christ, abiding in him, is a gospel-enabled journey, a planted seed that keeps growing.

He works in us, through us, and often, *in spite of* us. He's the Greatest Honeyguide who clearly doesn't need our help. But mercy of mercies, he still chooses to fly to our doorstep and say "Follow me." He wants us to move in the same direction he does. He calls us to participate in his kingdom purposes, to get our hands (and opposable thumbs) knuckle-deep into the sweetness of his life-giving intentions for this world.

Whittle While You Work

Over the years, I've acquired an odd assemblage of figurines I refer to as my "Ducks of the World Collection." It started in Mexico with a pair of earthenware ducks I bought on a whim in a restaurant gift shop. I never intended it to get out of hand, but (as tends to happen) like attracts like, and one weird knickknack quickly becomes two, then three, and the next thing you know, you've got a collection. Ducks are fairly ubiquitous, making random duck figurines easier to acquire than you might imagine (just in case you're looking to start a duck collection of your own). In my various travels, I've acquired etched brass ducks from India, a carved soapstone duck from Panama, and mosaic tile ducks from Spain. But my hands-down favorite is my Canadian duck. It's a small wooden rendition of a merganser, hand-carved by a retired Royal Canadian Mountie from a piece of beaver-chewed alderwood from the northernmost shores of Lake Huron in Ontario. By my count that's at least a million Canada points; simply holding it will make you start singing "O Canada, our home and native land." You can still see the beaver teeth marks in it.

I've always thought it would be an impressive thing to be a driftwood sculptor—to look at some gnawed branch and think, "I know what I can make out of that." The eye of an artist can look at an unglamorous beginning and see a beautiful end. I think about this wooden duck when I think about God's work in me and my work in him. After all, I was once a piece of chewed-up driftwood, fit for firewood at best. God saw something different—an image he intended to restore and complete, a dead heart made new, a stick snatched from the fire. That's his work.

What's *my* work? To cooperate with the process of whittling. Bringing ducks out of driftwood requires sawing, cutting, carving, chiseling, shaping, sanding, smoothing, treating, varnishing. I'm not suggesting that any of that will be pleasant. God disciplines those he loves (Hebrews 12:6). He prunes our branches to bear more fruit (John 15:2). So your work, dear reader, is to embrace the blade. Your work is to glorify the artist and trust the process of the art, knowing that he is working even now to perfect us into the image of Jesus Christ.

Michelangelo's statue of David was carved from a twelve-ton block of marble that was judged by other sculptors to be defective. The stone lay abandoned for almost forty years before Michelangelo took up the challenge, and his capacity to create the perfect sculpture from flawed materials is still hailed today as the greatest achievement in sculpture the world has ever known. At its unveiling, one patron is said to have asked, "How could you have possibly achieved a masterpiece like this from such a crude slab of marble?" Though likely apocryphal, Michelangelo purportedly said, "Simple. All I did was chip away everything that didn't look like David, until only he remained."

One day the Lord will say to his people, without a hint of sarcasm, "I have chipped away from you everything that didn't look like Jesus, until only he remains." Our character will be perfectly conformed to his. God is committed to perfecting the image of Christ in his people. At any point in our journey, he already sees the finished work of Christ established in us. While we can't yet see that finished work, we can trust his process. Elsewhere, Paul writes, "We are his workmanship, created in Christ Jesus for good works, which God prepared beforehand, that we should walk in them" (Ephesians 2:10, ESV). We're not saved by works, but we *are* his work, a trophy of grace, an artistic rendering of the image of Christ himself. He has saved us for this. And amazingly, he has destined good works for us to contribute to his kingdom-building purposes.

The path for that work is built by small decisions of obedience, starting right now, continuing tomorrow, until our final breath. We walk *with* him, letting him lead, applying our hands and feet to our faith. He gifts us the desire and ability to do so.

Circling back to that little bird in Africa, it's not a stretch to say that honey awaits. After all, God's promise to his people was a land flowing with milk and honey. We await the day when we will savor the sweetness of our promised land. And we have a Savior, the Greatest Honeyguide, to lead us there.

— CHAPTER 8 —

A Bird Mascot for the Church

Do everything without grumbling or arguing, so that you may become blameless and pure, "children of God without fault in a warped and crooked generation." Then you will shine among them like stars in the sky as you hold firmly to the word of life.

—PHILIPPIANS 2:14–16

The method of the kingdom will match the message of the kingdom. The kingdom will come as the church, energized by the Spirit, goes out into the world vulnerable, suffering, praising, praying, misunderstood, misjudged, vindicated, celebrating: always… bearing in the body the dying of Jesus so that the life of Jesus may also be displayed.

—N. T. WRIGHT[1]

EVERYONE LOVES A good bird mascot.

Kentucky was the first U.S. state to designate an official state bird, claiming the Northern Cardinal in 1926. By 1970 every state had followed suit with their own pick. But bird mascots predate the United States by several hundred years. The impressive Golden Eagle, for instance, has represented Mexico since at least 1821, and Germany since 1433. And ravens adorned Viking shields and banners as far back as the ninth century. In more recent cultural icons, five NFL teams and three Major League Baseball teams claim bird mascots (eleven if we count their minor league farm teams like the Rochester Red Wings, Toledo Mud Hens, and Down East Wood Ducks). NBC has its peacock, San Diego has its chicken, and Aflac has its duck.

Have you ever wondered what might make a good bird mascot for the church? Presbyterians like me might relate well to the Carolina Wren: easily agitated, very verbose, tail lifted like a stiff caution flag, and eyebrows always raised. Frankly, it looks a little uptight, like it just got back from our general assembly. Perhaps the Baptists would gravitate to a diving duck like the Hooded Merganser: the sort of bird that's most comfortable in an environment that allows full immersion. The Northern Cardinal might make a great mascot for Pentecostals: a little red tongue of fire and the first one singing in the morning, with the stamina to keep going well into the afternoon.

But what about a bird for the church universal? Is there a bird that represents the mission we're called to and the role we're made to play in this world? The Bible has a lot to say about our mission. Salt and light. City on a hill. In the world but not of it. Love thy neighbor. Go into all the world. Scripture depicts our cultural engagement with many different images, and if we wrote a manifesto for the church's call, we'd need to incorporate all of these ideas into the discussion. And yet when we put them all on paper, we realize that some of these exhortations seem to conflict with each other. For example, a city on a hill might be aloof and unapproachable, neglecting neighborly engagement. The call to be the salt of the earth feels at odds with the command to be in the world but not of it. The Bible contains both the call to be separate and the picture of becoming all things to all people. So, which is it?

Today the church still struggles to get this right, often losing its bearings as we swing from heavy-handed to hands-off. So let's consider four common approaches, and (in the spirit of ornitheology) illustrate each with a bird.

1. The Penguin: Church Apart from Culture

Down at the bottom of our globe, in the forbidding chill of a remote hunk of rock called South Georgia Island, there's a city that's growing exponentially. The human contingent on the island—in the best of circumstances—numbers only about thirty, mostly an assortment of scientists. But the city I'm referring to, just over the bluff, totals over four hundred thousand, and everyone's wearing a tuxedo.

City is not too strong a word for this astounding colony of King Penguins: These waddling city planners have created walking thoroughfares, hospitals, supermarkets, green space, and daycare centers. Filmmakers bring in their widest-angle lenses and highest-flying drones to capture the immensity of it all. Urban life in Penguin City is flourishing—a booming metropolis where just one hundred years ago, less than a thousand birds gathered.

Who doesn't like penguins? They walk with royal dignity and a hint of stand-up comedian. They brave long distances and ridiculous weather to raise their young and protect their tribe. They dive to one hundred meters, walk seventy miles, thrive at ten below, and somehow keep a positive attitude, to all outward appearances at least.

And yet all of this happens in isolation—a world tucked away from all other species. Aside from the occasional skua or seal, the penguins have largely cordoned themselves off from the world. Unless you're a nature documentary producer, their life has no real bearing upon yours; they exist as a literal island.

In terms of penguin ecology, this monoculture is probably for the best, but my point is this: If a Christian's primary motif of cultural connection is "come out and be separate," the church will remain distinct at the expense of its witness. We will retreat when we're called to advance. And we don't have to move to the Antarctic to do so. We can ghetto off into a Christian subculture that only reads Christian books and only listens to Christian music and only watches Christian movies and only drinks Christian milk from Christian cows owned by Christian farmers we found in the Christian yellow pages. Maybe it's safe on the island, but in the end, we are abdicating.

And when we abdicate, we voluntarily go exactly where the world already wants us to be: disengaged from the public sphere, hidden safely behind the barricade Peter Berger calls an "innocuous 'play area,'"[2] stripped of any real potential for influence. We've interpreted the concept of the separation of church and state to imagine faith should be a quiet, private thing, fine as a side hobby as long as we never speak of it in public. But the intent of America's founding fathers was to prevent a faith *imposed,* not a faith *expressed.*

I was recently summoned for jury duty and was being examined as a potential juror when one of the attorneys found out I was a pastor. He immediately expressed his flustered concern and asked if I was able to set aside my beliefs to render a good verdict. I said no, I couldn't, because my beliefs are what *motivate* my commitment to render a good verdict, believing a just God desires just decisions. Apparently, this was not the right answer, unless the question was "What's the quickest way to get dismissed from a jury pool?" The world around us says faith is fine as long as it doesn't influence your policy if you're in government, your decisions if you're in law, or your morals if you're a teacher. Keep your faith on the island, somewhere far away and cold.

When we cordon off our faith to a Christian subculture, we've moved to Penguin City. We might thrive there, but the world will never know.

2. The Potoo: Church Indistinguishable from Culture

If our Costa Rican river guide didn't know exactly where to look, there's no chance I would have seen this bird. We were meandering down a calm section of the Rio Sarapiquí in a flat-bottomed boat, binoculars at the ready as our guide pointed out sloths, monkeys, iguanas, and other flora and fauna of La Selva Biological Reserve. Both shores teemed with all sorts of exotic finds. But now, cautiously and carefully, the boat eased toward the south shoreline and our guide excitedly gestured toward... a stump. One of my friends mumbled his disappointment: "Great. A stump." But the guide shook his head, pointed again more forcefully, and whispered, "Grán pooo-toooo." The stump tapered to a point, a sort of gnarled snag, a scraggly finger pointing upward.

And then the snag opened one eye.

The Great Potoo isn't rare in the sense of being endangered; the population in Central and South America is actually very healthy. They're just rare to see—not only because the potoo is nocturnal, but because it's unbelievably talented at blending in.

The bird exudes the essence of bark, in hue and pattern, and when it sits on the end of a branch, neck extended, eyes closed, you'll be hard-pressed to figure out where the tree ends and the bird begins. It can sit this way all day, imperceptible in its movements, perfect in its camouflage. In its non-stealth mode, perched on, say, a fence post, it's an easy ID, shaped like a buggy-eyed Muppet with an enormous mouth capable of frighteningly haunting screams. But when it's done shrieking, it's back to the branch—neck up, eyes closed, vanishing in plain sight.

The potoo's basic life strategy is to blend in. God's people throughout history have attempted similar approaches. Israel in the time of the monarchy struggled with a desire to be like the surrounding nations, adopting their practices, shrines, and worship rituals. Conformity is much less awkward, isn't it? That's why we're tempted to do the same thing today, imitating the latest trends and redefining controversial beliefs to sound more palatable. Sadly, when we take our marching orders from the surrounding marketplace of ideas, the distinctive message and witness of the church is lost. Sure, we might sound less peculiar and more accommodating, but in the process, we develop a sort of laryngitis for truth. Avoiding the discomfort of words like *sin, salvation, heaven,* and *hell* might tame the gospel's more shocking aspects, but in doing so, we barter away some high-stakes life-and-death realities and exchange them for the relevance of the latest cultural trend, trying to march in step with the social status quo. The world needs a more courageous witness—comfortably communicating the uncomfortable. Author Russell Moore warns, "A Christianity that is without friction in the culture is a Christianity that dies."[3] Sitting on the latest cultural stump, it becomes hard to distinguish where the branch ends and the bird begins.

Both the penguin and the potoo dissociate from engaging with the culture. In one case, we lose proximity to those who need a message of grace; in the other, we lose the message itself.

So here's a totally different approach: What if the solution is to move in really close and yell really loud?

3. The Blue Jay: Church Attacking Culture

Philippians 2:14 says, "Do everything without grumbling or arguing." Tell that to a Blue Jay.

The jay is a featherweight boxer ready to rumble. Famously aggressive and fiercely territorial, it's committed to total domination at any backyard feeder. In chapter 6, I mentioned the study on bird interaction in North America, the one where the Brown Creeper got ranked at the bottom. The Blue Jay, on the other hand, was ranked near the top, in the upper echelons of bird aggression, unapologetically running off almost all other species. Its call isn't a song as much as a scold, letting the whole neighborhood in on its angst. It also employs outright deception; Blue Jays can imitate the call of a Red-shouldered Hawk so effectively that even the best birders often can't tell the difference. A hawk shriek definitely clears out a feeder quickly, making space for hungry jays. I'm reminded of the middle school punks who ruled my school cafeteria, swiping french fries and pizza slices from helpless victims. No one was happy while they were still hungry, and wow, they ate a *lot.*

Many backyard birdwatchers disdain jays almost as much as jays seem to disdain the world. When a jay is in your feeder, you're not apt to see much else, as other species run for cover. At the same time, it's hard to deny the beauty of a Blue Jay, with feathers radiating the perfect hue of steely blue, crisply trimmed in sharp whites and blacks, and topped with a valiant crest. Sketched in a field guide, they exude a handsome photogenic luster. But as poet Frank Bolles wrote, "All his beauty is delusion, / All his tricks are tricks of darkness."[4] How can a bird be so beautifully annoying and yet so annoyingly beautiful?

The cultural-engagement script for many Christians goes something like this: "Once upon a time we *had* the culture, but then we *lost* the culture, and now we need to fight to get the culture *back*." We reflect on better days when Christian morality was the norm—when our perspective was welcome at the center of the national cultural identity. And when we see a very different landscape today, in which our convictions seem marginalized, we embrace the Blue Jay's in-it-to-win-it scrappiness. We take to our keyboards to engage the critics, mock their shallow contradictions, and defend the faith with gusto. We turn to political saviors and combative social media threads—tools that arguably were never the church's to wield in the first place. In our attempts to turn the tide, we make strange alliances: "The enemy of my enemy is my friend." Often driven by fear more than faith (if we're honest with ourselves), we strive to win back the culture at all costs. It's us versus them.

What possibly starts with good intentions can quickly escalate into a message of anger, fear, or belligerence, all in the name of a gospel message of compassion, hope, and forgiveness. The result is confusing, weakening rather than strengthening the Christian message, and the world cries "hypocrite." We easily forget our faith is rooted in the weakness of a crucified Savior who calls us to engage the world with meekness, gentleness, lowliness, and a compassionate, others-first message. Yelling may win the argument, while forfeiting things that are far more important: credibility, integrity, and grace. Shouldn't the method demonstrate the message?

Here's a thought to lower the temperature of our argumentative hearts: Those who deny the faith and attack the faithful aren't enemies to be defeated—they're part of the mission itself. When we remember this—no longer hoping to win arguments but to win hearts—we may find ourselves more coherently communicating the beautiful hope of our Savior.

Yes, there's plenty of hostility in the culture around us, tempting us to fight or flee. Penguin and potoo Christians choose the flight option, penguins withdrawing to a safe island subculture and potoos hiding in plain sight. Jay Christians fight back, determined to reclaim ground. But what if God has put us in this world, at this specific place and time, for a much better purpose?

The Kingdom of God Is Like . . .

We could certainly propose other birds that might portray the role of the church in the world: the conquering eagle, for instance, or the sacrificial dove, or the wise owl. There are aspects of truth in these images. And to be clear, there are also aspects of truth in the three birds I've already mentioned because there are moments when all three of these approaches inform our calling.

Yes, penguin lovers, sometimes we are called to come out and be separate (2 Corinthians 6:14–18 or 1 John 2:15, for example). Yes, there is a certain amount of potoo-inspired "blending in" as we relate to people for the sake of communicating gospel truth, becoming "all things to all people" (1 Corinthians 9:22). And yes, there are times when we need to speak out and defend the truth with Blue Jay boldness (Galatians 2:11; Titus 1:10–11).

But as our defining matrix for engaging the world, I'm convinced there's a nobler image. What if, as we seek an appropriate bird mascot for the church's role in the world, we think on a smaller scale? After all, Jesus encouraged us to "think small" in our understanding of how the kingdom of God advances.

With the entirety of the natural world to draw his illustrations from, he zeroed in on microscopic items like mustard seeds, pearls, and a bit of yeast—little things with big impact. So, following Jesus's examples, what tiny bird might offer the best glimpse of the church's role in the world?

Consider the hummingbird.

4. The Hummingbird: Church Transforming Culture

The average hummingbird weighs about a tenth of an ounce. Put three paper clips in your hand and you'll understand what a tenth of an ounce feels like—it's practically weightless. And yet this minuscule bird is capable of miraculous things. It can hover in place for over ninety minutes. It can shoot across a cul-de-sac at thirty miles an hour and brake to an instant stop on the tiny target of an azalea bloom. A hummingbird's flight muscles make up 80 percent of its weight and flap its wings in an artistic figure eight up to one hundred times per second. Per *second.* (By comparison, a wood duck does just fine at about seven beats per second). The hummingbird's amazing muscles are powered by a pea-sized heart that—relative to the bird's size—is the largest in the animal kingdom and can beat up to 1,200 times a minute.[5] In fact, in their nightly torpor—a rest so deep the bird often appears dead—their heart still clips away at up to two hundred beats per minute. It's as if their heart refuses to admit it needs a nap.

Have you considered, though, that a hummingbird isn't just a marvel of nature but a transformer of it? Hummingbirds are among the most efficient pollinators in the world. Those crazy-fast wingbeats create tons of turbulence, kicking up pollen to spread about, and catching plenty of it within the minuscule hooks that keep a feather's barbs in tandem. Some plants are adapted to hummingbird-only specifications, relying on their long beaks and rapid-fire tongues to reach deep into a flower's nectar. And their hyperactive lifestyle equates to hundreds of flower visits in the course of a day: A bloom can count on its pollen getting some bonus frequent-flier miles.

A hummingbird's mere presence helps its environment to flourish. Its daily actions transform the world around it, bringing a flourishing life and health. Imagine the impact of ordinary believers committed to transforming their spheres of influence, the places where they live and learn and work and play, carrying the pollen of a different sort of kingdom. Imagine God's people—the cultivation of the Spirit's ripening fruit—bringing the realities of "thy kingdom come" to a wilting world. When the Lord returns, heavenly realities will become earthly ones as God makes all things new. Awaiting that day, we seek to be responsible to those realities. A perfect future justice motivates today's pursuit of just laws. A total future healing motivates today's pursuit of compassionate medicine, counseling, and caregiving. Most of all, the future experience of a world centered on the throne of grace motivates us to declare clearly the completed work of Jesus Christ and to call others to surrender to his lordship. Every occupation, pursuit, and service is an opportunity to cross-pollinate.

What does this have to do with Philippians 2? When Paul exhorts his Philippian friends to engage their culture, he calls them to be "blameless and pure, 'children of God without fault in a warped and crooked generation.' Then you will shine among them like stars in the sky as you hold firmly to the word of life" (Philippians 2:15–16). This exhortation has hummingbird hope in it. Paul acknowledges the crooked nature of a godless culture, and yet he counsels them to neither a jay fight nor a penguin flight. He also cautions them against the cultural compromise of potoo camouflage.

Instead he tells them to shine like stars. Paul pictures a host of starry lights, each one a believer who is faithfully living an intentional life with transformative outcomes. Our call is to bring warm light to a world in darkness—making the invisible kingdom visible.

Let Your Light Shine

As I commend to us the hummingbird, I'm reminded of a Native American myth about the creation of the night sky.[6] As the story opens, the animals of the world are living in disharmony and bickering, and the Great Spirit responds by throwing a blanket over the canopy of the world, consigning it to total darkness. The animals gather a council to determine how to tear down the blanket and reveal the sun again. The great bear goes first, jumping to his full height and swiping with his claws, but he only succeeds in tearing a few scratches, explaining the formation of the Milky Way (and his fall to the earth, landing on his posterior, accounts for his stubby tail).

Next comes the vulture, the great king of the sky, who soars high to rip down the blanket with his beak. He only succeeds in punching through the blanket with his head, creating a circular hole of light. The moon is thus formed, and in the process, the heat of the sun sears off the vulture's head feathers, explaining why vultures today are bald.

But last comes a drab little bird who hovers to the roof of the sky and begins poking small holes with his tiny beak. Each hole only lets through a dim shaft of light, but the bird continues poking, filling the entire sky with holes and eventually collapsing from the monumental exertion. His act of heroism saves the day; the Great Spirit sees the animals working together and agrees on a compromise, lifting the blanket to give day and replacing it, holes and all, to create night. He also rewards the small drab bird with the vibrant colors of royalty. In this legend, it's the hummingbird that creates the stars.

It's just a fun myth, mind you, but the Bible agrees on this much: God changes the world in big ways through small moves. A minuscule mustard seed, a puny pearl, a trifling amount of yeast . . . and maybe the tiny travels of the world's smallest bird. This is how the kingdom of God moves forward. Our hummingbird faithfulness is a light to the world's darkness. Our journey of faithfulness (and even, Paul says in verse 14, our conviction not to argue) will star-shine the night sky.

But don't miss the source. Jesus said, "I am the light of the world. Whoever follows me will never walk in darkness, but will have the light of life" (John 8:12). It's the monumental exertion of *Jesus*—even to a cross and beyond—that has poked a hole in our wayward hearts and allowed light to shine through. It's *his* light, not ours. But as we live intentionally, asking him to reveal himself through us, he will use those small lights to transform the world.

— CHAPTER 9 —

The Contentions & Courtesies of Crows

For everyone looks out for their own interests, not those of Jesus Christ. But you know that Timothy has proved himself.

—PHILIPPIANS 2:21–22

I plead with Euodia and I plead with Syntyche to be of the same mind in the Lord.

—PHILIPPIANS 4:2

I never forget a face—but I'm going to make an exception in your case.

—GROUCHO MARX[1]

ON A STONE building on the University of Washington campus, a resident crow nicknamed Bela sits with his bird family, watching the comings and goings of students on the lawn below. From the crowd he spots a blond-headed woman named Lijana whom he immediately recognizes as his breakfast buddy. He flies to the lamppost above Lijana, who offers him her usual meat-and-eggs meal cooked especially for him. She calls him by name, and he calmly hops down to enjoy another delightful breakfast with his human friend.

Later that morning, back up on his perch again, Bela spots another recognizable face, a wildlife science professor named John Marzluff, whose research team was responsible for affixing an identification band to Bela's leg five and a half years ago. Bela didn't appreciate it then, and he still hasn't gotten over it. He breaks into a rage-induced scream and jumps from his perch to go dive-bomb the professor. His family takes flight to join in the attack, along with other neighboring crows, circling and scolding and taking aerial passes at the professor. Marzluff's presence has turned the campus lawn into a Hitchcock movie. Says Marzluff, "We wonder when, or if, he will ever forget (or forgive) us."[2]

In Paul's letter to the Philippians, four supporting cast members are mentioned in two pairings. Two of them showcase a capacity to give; the other two showcase an incapacity to *for*give. The crow has a lesson to teach us regarding both.

Unforgettable

Numerous studies agree: Crows remember faces. That's a pleasant thought if you're one of those sorts of people who cook breakfast for crows. But it's unsettling if you've ever done anything to tick one off, because a crow never forgets. Not only do they remember the face of a human they don't like, but they pass that information along to their fellow crows, and even to their offspring. And considering an estimated world population of thirty million crows, it's sobering to imagine the lingering grudge of an angry flock. Crows are the ultimate in cancel culture.

Do you remember when Jesus warned that our secret indiscretions will one day "be proclaimed from the roofs" (Luke 12:3)? Well, check the roof and you might see a crow up there, instigating his fellow birds to spread the news of your misdeeds. That goes double for the words you speak, according to Solomon:

> Do not revile the king even in your thoughts,
> or curse the rich in your bedroom,
> because a bird in the sky may carry your words,
> and a bird on the wing may report what you say.
> (Ecclesiastes 10:20)

If you've read Suzanne Collins's *The Ballad of Songbirds and Snakes,* you know that this verse would have been a helpful warning for poor Sejanus Plinth. Long before *The Hunger Games* invented the jabberjay, Solomon knew that a bird can get you in trouble.

Back on campus in Seattle, Marzluff has documented multiple studies utilizing rubber masks that crows associate with a "bad" person, such as a researcher who fiddled around with their nest or (heaven forbid) tried to ID-band them. Regardless of variety in clothing, hats, or the person involved, the presence of that one particular mask unleashes a torrent of crow wrath. For many of the birds, the aggressive heckling isn't even based on firsthand experience; they simply (to borrow from an REO Speedwagon tune) "heard it from a friend who heard it from a friend who heard it from another, you've been messin' around."[3] In the years since the mask experiment was first introduced in 2006, the crow mob has grown exponentially, largely made up of birds that personally never witnessed anything amiss from that strange masked man.[4] But ask any crow at the University of Washington, and—if you could speak crow, of course—they'd tell you not to trust that guy. (It's worth mentioning that since the mask looks vaguely like Michael Myers from the *Halloween* movie franchise, a lot of the humans on campus probably feel the same way.)

Your reputation precedes you. At least with crows.

In Philippians 4:2, Paul writes, "I plead with Euodia and I plead with Syntyche to be of the same mind in the Lord." Although this letter is probably the most positive and issue-free book in the New Testament, it still hints at internal tensions. Notice how Paul has been exhorting unity? Otherscenteredness? Humility? If you flip back through the prior chapters of this book, you'll realize that these themes of albatross commitment, starling cooperation, and treecreeper humility aren't topics being brought up in a vacuum. And now Paul addresses the elephant in the room.

We'll never know what these two women were arguing about, but if you've been in a church for any length of time, you know there's no shortage of contentious churchy topics. Perhaps they were arguing about whether the Communion bread should be gluten-free. Or whether the drums were too loud. Or whether the youth director should be asked to wear a collared shirt on Sundays. Maybe Euodia can't fathom why Syntyche would vote for so-and-so, or send her kids to public school, or repost that article on Facebook. Okay, admittedly, I might be projecting my own experiences. Guilty. But whatever they were arguing about, it was worthy of three chapters about commitment, perspective, unity, mission, and humility.

Clearly these two women were gospel-minded co-laboring

servants of the church, because in verse 3 Paul says that "they have contended at my side in the cause of the gospel." But they've allowed this dispute to wreak havoc on not only their friendship but the health of the church. Overstated, perhaps? I don't think so. The volatility of this situation had become a public matter, and Paul even suggests a mediator might be warranted—the unnamed "true companion" of verse 3. In my experience as a pastor, I've seen enough discord to know that it only takes two people to tear a whole church apart.

This doesn't mean the argument between Euodia and Syntyche was unimportant, although sometimes our disputes can be so. Surprisingly though, notice that Paul doesn't take sides. He urges them to be "of the same mind," without lobbying for either Euodia's mind or Syntyche's mind. Don't you find it interesting that we're never told what the point of contention was? Paul didn't need to elaborate, nor did God want later readers of this letter to get off topic by choosing sides. The issue, whatever it was, wasn't the issue. For Paul, the *most* important thing was for his friends to be "of the same mind in the Lord."

What does that look like? Rewind the tape. Paul has already prayed for their love to be rooted in knowledge and for their discernment (Philippians 1:9–10). He's called them to strive together as one and to exhibit conduct that's worthy of the gospel (1:27). He's challenged them to a deeper humility (2:5–8) and warned them to avoid complaining and arguing (2:14). He's cautioned against self-interest (2:3, 21) and self-righteousness (3:7–9). In fact, he's already challenged them to be "of the same mind" with a fuller definition of what that means. Chapter 2 starts this way:

> Therefore if you have any encouragement from being united with Christ, if any comfort from his love, if any common sharing in the Spirit, if any tenderness and com-

passion, then make my joy complete by being like-minded, having the same love, being one in spirit *and of one mind.* (Philippians 2:1–2)

Paul shows us where being "of one mind" comes from. Like-mindedness is fueled by the encouragement of our union with Christ, our comfort from his love, and our compassion for others. Those realities torpedo our arrogance and ambition and exhort us to put others first (2:3–4). In short, to have the mind of Christ is to get out of our own head—to let our relationship with Jesus motivate everything we do.

What if God wants us to be *Christlike* more than he wants us to be *right*? What if the issue isn't the real issue? What if the greatest need is to exemplify Jesus within our disagreements? What ticking bombs in your own heart could be defused by that reality?

It's often said, "I'll forgive but I won't forget." As a pastor, if I had a dollar for every time I've heard that sentiment invoked in a counseling session, I could seriously upgrade my birding binoculars. It's a common conviction, but frankly I still haven't found the chapter and verse it comes from. We prefer to maintain our crow-on-a-rooftop vigilance, ready to sound the alarm when the guilty party shows its face. Notwithstanding the need for wisdom and setting boundaries, forgiveness is a heart issue, and the unwillingness to forget is part of the poison.

I remember an extended family gathering years ago, sitting around the kitchen table as my aunt put the milk back in the refrigerator. "Oh no you don't!" cried another aunt, swooping hurriedly into the room. "We all remember what happened *last* year when you spilled it everywhere!" Personally, I didn't. But she did. A crow never forgets.

For a moment, picture yourself as a second- or third-generation Seattle-raised crow. You've been squawking at that odd masked man on campus your whole life, because your crow ancestors told you it was the right thing to do. But imagine the moment of lucidity when you turn to your current generation of fellow crows and say, "Yeah, but really, why are we doing this?" and you all discover that no one really knows. Whatever the issue once was, it's been forgotten. You're free to stop squawking now.

Busybody that I am, I'd really love to know what Euodia and Syntyche were arguing about. When I get to heaven and ask them, though, I have a feeling they might both say, "You know what? I can't remember." Grace is that good.

Crows Bearing Gifts

A few miles down the road from Bela and the campus crows, Gary Clark assembles a messy pile of leftovers on a backyard TV tray. He mixes some raw chicken and old pizza with dry dog food and peanuts, a daily ration for his local crows. The sound of dog kibble on the metal tray acts as a dinner bell, and within minutes a few dozen crows arrive. Gary has been doing this routine since 2004, and the birds are well-accustomed to him. But the relationship took a more reciprocal turn just after Valentine's Day 2006. Gary jokingly said to the assembled flock, "Hey, how come you never bring *me* anything? I always give you food, and you never bring me anything." He left the birds to their meal. But when he returned later to clean the empty tray, he discovered a small purple heart placed at the center of it—the hard sugary candy we give out on Valentine's Day. It still bore the inscription: "Love."[5]

John Marzluff (the professor we met at the beginning of this chapter) has checked the story out, and as one who studies crows for a living, he's convinced Gary's not making this up. In fact, his experience aligns with numerous other incidents between crows and humans, several of which Marzluff cites in his book *Gifts of the Crow.*[6] A Missouri woman regularly receives shards of colored glass in her feeder. Another woman from Indiana was sitting outside reading a book in her yard when a crow landed in her lap, dropped a wooden bead in it, and flew off. Yet another brought a shiny house key. Quite a gift, if only the recipient knew which house it belonged to.

In 2015, an eight-year-old girl named Gabi Mann began feeding her lunch leftovers to crows on her walk home from the school bus stop. When the crows started waiting for her and following her all the way home, she asked her mom if they could set up a food tray in the backyard. One morning Gabi noticed a trinket carefully placed on the tray. In the coming weeks, random treasures began appearing: bolts and screws, earrings, buttons, random plastic objects, and Gabi's personal favorite, a pearl-colored heart charm.[7] One day, while Gabi's mom Lisa was trying to get some Bald Eagle photos, she dropped her camera lens in a nearby alley. The next day she found it sitting neatly alongside the bird bath. When Lisa played back her home security footage, she was astonished to see the crow rinse it off for her.[8]

What do we make of these treasures? Is it admiration? Gratitude? A tip for good service? These crows behave in a way that's unexpected yet very intentional. The action requires forethought and multiple steps, like a human strolling the mall looking for the perfect gift for that special someone.

While it's true that the crow's capacity for facial recognition enables them to hold grudges, it also creates the possibility of a giving relationship. These crows exhibit behavior that we don't fully understand but that might be best described as *thoughtfulness.* Unlike Euodia and Syntyche, when Paul references his second pair of friends, we see an inspiring selflessness. Timothy and Epaphroditus live thoughtfully for others, leaving a trail of intentional gifts behind them.

Ordinary Faithfulness

In one sense, neither of these men receive more than an honorable mention on the roll call of faith. There are far more memorable characters: Peter has a jailbreak, Paul's gym towels heal the sick, and Philip teleports mysteriously from one place to another. By comparison, Timothy is an average-Joe character, not connected to any recorded wow moments and yet faithfully present throughout the story of the early church. He was with Paul in Galatia, Philippi, and Berea. He helped establish the church in Thessalonica. He was a messenger for Paul in Athens, Ephesus, Corinth, and Rome, eventually pastoring the Ephesian church. He's the recipient of two personal letters in Scripture, including Paul's final recorded words. And tradition holds that he died a martyr's death. But all of this occurred without any fanfare: The Bible doesn't record a single thing Timothy said. He's presented as a dutiful background character. And Epaphroditus is even more "background" than that, somewhere near the bottom of the movie credits. He's only mentioned here in Philippians.

That's why I love these two guys. Somehow their down-to-earth service feels more accessible, more grounded in the realities of daily Christian living. Their record of service doesn't include miraculous earthquakes or angelic visions—just simple faithfulness, seen through mail deliveries, prison visits, and ordinary compassion. They portray the heart of a shepherd with the dutifulness of a UPS driver. For a twenty-first-century disciple, doesn't that example feel more . . . *attainable*?

Paul introduces Epaphroditus to us as "my brother, co-worker and fellow soldier, who is also your messenger, whom you sent to take care of my needs" (Philippians 2:25). As a high schooler discovering the Bible for the first time, I read about Epaphroditus in a Sunday school class and decided that he was my new favorite Bible hero. Partly, I'm sure, I was just trying to pick an obscure, nonconformist answer (in case I was asked who my favorite Bible character was, as high school teens are wont to ask). But Epaphroditus really did impress me, and it was verse 26 that drew my respect: "For he longs for all of you and is distressed because you heard he was ill." Shouldn't that read, "He is distressed because he's ill"? Seriously, if I'm sick, I'm playing the sympathy card, staying home from school, and seizing on my mom's pity to get some consoling service—like endless saltine crackers and ginger ale with the bubbles stirred out. How Mom might be feeling in that moment—worried or tired or having to miss work—was not on my radar. How in the world could a guy be sick and selfless at the same time, worried at the impact his illness might have on others? Epaphroditus was "sick unto death" (which, in the days prior to modern medicine, generally meant "death"). In a situation like that, he's focused on others, concerned for the effect of his absence on his church back home in Philippi.

Timothy's others-mindedness is equally commendable. Paul writes, "I have no one else like him, who will show genuine concern for your welfare. For everyone looks out for their own interests, not those of Jesus Christ. But you know that Timothy has proved himself, because as a son with his father he has served with me in the work of the gospel" (Philippians 2:20–22). Unlike other would-be missionaries like Diotrephes "who loves to be first" (3 John 9) or Demas who "loved this world" (2 Timothy 4:10), Timothy's got his priorities sorted out. The result is a selfless capacity to serve the Philippians, Paul, and whoever else might cross his path. Whatever the opposite of narcissism is, it looks like this.

Neither Timothy nor Epaphroditus is noted for big highlight-reel plays or sensational acts of devotion. They're commended for their daily faithfulness, the accumulation of daily trinkets left at the bird feeder, a life of gratitude lived out in the little things.

Go and do likewise.

But is that too mundane for us? Maybe we'd prefer to be known for the sensational moment, the big sacrificial move. After all, we tend to spend 99 percent of our lives waiting for the next big thing to happen—the next benchmark or achievement: graduations and weddings and promotions and retirements. Those are nice. But *life* happens in the 99 percent. And *that* is where we're called to selfless faithfulness.

Sure, parents, if tomorrow you were faced with the contrived scenario of either quitting your job or losing your family, I hope the choice would be obvious. But how have you chosen your family over your job in your actions this week? If a game show host gave you the choice of funding a third-world orphanage or taking home a new sofa, I'd like to think that most of you would give your winnings to the kids (even if just to save face on national TV). But how have you chosen compassion over possessions in your decisions this month? The decisions we face, in which we're put to the test, are far smaller. And *far more important.* The one who is faithful with little will be faithful with much (Luke 16:10).

Little Gabi Mann (now a young adult) has a unique collection of crow gifts, filed away in plastic organizers. None of them are valuable or sensational, but as a whole they represent a unique relationship. They are daily deposits of affection, symbols that say, "Someone was thinking of me today." This assembling of random screws and coins and heart charms is far more than the sum of its parts. For the crows—as much as we understand the inner workings of a crow, at least—it sure looks a lot like gratitude.

Gratitude is what motivates our daily deposits as well, small trinkets accumulated over time that say, "Thanks for feeding me. Thanks for serving me. Thanks for giving yourself for me." For the Christian, all that gratitude is directed toward Christ, with the added blessing "Thanks for forgiving me."

Can a bird understand this? Perhaps. Author Mark Winter recounts the story of Cuthbert, the Celtic saint of Northumbria. A pair of ravens (see chapter 16) had shredded his thatched roof while pillaging for nest materials. He scolded them and told them to leave his island, which they obediently did. Three days later one of them returned, approaching Cuthbert with his head hung low in a posture that looked surprisingly like repentance. Cuthbert told the raven that he was forgiven and that he and his mate were welcome to return. The pair came back the next day, each one with a piece of hardened pig's lard that they laid at Cuthbert's feet as a gift.[9]

I know what you're thinking. Pig's lard is a lousy gift. Actually, it's apparently very handy for greasing the shoes of seventh-century monks, but that's not the point. We who are guilty of pillaging the roof have been declared forgiven. What better reason to say thank you with daily deposits of ordinary faithfulness? After all, Jesus had every reason to focus on the pain of the cross but instead looked like Epaphroditus in thinking of others: "Father, forgive them, for they do not know what they are doing" (Luke 23:34). He had every reason to look to his own interests but instead looked like Timothy in prioritizing his flock's need and his Father's will.

More accurately, Jesus didn't look like Epaphroditus and Timothy. They looked like him. In our life lived from gratitude, we can do the same. What daily deposits can we lay before the One who cares for us so well?

— CHAPTER 10 —

Bowerbird Treasures

Whatever were gains to me I now consider loss for the sake of Christ. What is more, I consider everything a loss because of the surpassing worth of knowing Christ Jesus my Lord, for whose sake I have lost all things. I consider them garbage, that I may gain Christ and be found in him, not having a righteousness of my own that comes from the law, but that which is through faith in Christ—the righteousness that comes from God on the basis of faith.

—PHILIPPIANS 3:7–9

The supreme happiness of life is the conviction that we are loved; loved for ourselves—say rather, loved in spite of ourselves.

—VICTOR HUGO[1]

SHAKESPEARE WROTE, "ALL that glisters is not gold."[2] True, sometimes it's blue instead.

The Satin Bowerbird compulsively arranges and rearranges his collection of twigs, lined up vertically in two impressively neat rows, giving the impression of two parallel picket fences. Not a stick is out of place, and the bowerbird methodically inspects his work like a homeowner striving for a yard-of-the-month award. In reality, he's hoping to win something far more valuable than that.

Despite the similar use of materials, the "bower" this bird is building isn't a nest (that will be the female's job, if he can woo one). Instead, this alleyway of sticks is nothing short of a concert stage where the bowerbird will perform a series of elaborate shows for prospective mates. Each of the twenty-seven species of bowerbirds in Australia and New Guinea has a unique shtick, from the seductive matador-esque dance of the Flame Bowerbird to the ostentatious mansion building of the Vogelkop Bowerbird. For his part, the Satin Bowerbird knows a couple of rudimentary college-freshman dance moves and has a singing voice that might be best described as the sound of an old camera rewinding a roll of film. But his true hope of landing a first date isn't about the song and dance or the fancy digs. For this particular species, it's all about the trophy case.

The Satin Bowerbird has a neurotic obsession with the color blue. Perhaps it's the bright violet iris of his eye or the sharp contrast blue makes against his purple-black plumage. For whatever reason, blue is his precious. His hope of impressing a mate lies in his ability to collect vividly blue trinkets. This isn't as easy as it might sound; the next time you're hiking, try scanning the forest floor for blue items and you'll find that nature can be pretty thrifty with that particular color.

Unknowingly, humankind has aided significantly in the bowerbird's treasure collection, turning residential districts and picnic areas into the equivalent of the California Gold Rush. The bowerbird brings to his storeroom treasures old and new (Matthew 13:52). Blue bottle caps (*Thanks, Dasani!*). Blue pen caps (*Thanks, BIC!*). Blue Nerf darts (*Thanks, Hasbro!*). Blue pacifiers (*Thanks, crying baby!*). If you live in bowerbird territory in Australia, think twice before sporting any blue on your key ring; these birds have been known to snag car keys right off a picnic table.

All this blue bling is hauled back to the bower and arranged artistically in front of the stick-flanked stage. The bowerbird is inexplicably precise in the arrangement of these items, trying different layouts like a bachelor rearranging the furniture in his apartment, experimenting with aesthetic options, seeking the perfect feng shui.

And now, here come the ladies. It would be an understatement to say that the female bowerbird is not easily impressed. She's incomprehensibly picky. Her default impression is disapproval, and if a single aspect of his treasure aesthetic isn't to her liking, she's off to the next suitor. Perhaps the pen cap should have been arranged perpendicularly to the Nerf dart? Or is the blue glass not catching the light to its best advantage? Were the car keys a bit over the top?

Whatever the cause, if the female sees something imperfect, however small, there's no way Mr. Bowerbird is getting her phone number. The male frantically moves a trinket slightly left or right, a desperate "Wait, wait, baby, come back!" She might. Or she might not. As the old Head & Shoulders shampoo ad once said (on a blue plastic bottle, no less), you never get a second chance to make a first impression.

Weighed and Found Wanting

Now, imagine yourself as this love-scorned male bowerbird. You've collected an extraordinary array of treasure, a bonanza of blue that's worthy of a lifetime achievement award. But no matter how well you arrange it, no matter how perfectly you present it, it's not enough. The cumulative effect of all your best efforts is met with the disapproving violet-eyed stare of the one you hope to impress. "You have been weighed on the scales and found wanting" (Daniel 5:27).

Chris Slaten, a musician who goes by the moniker Son of Laughter, wrote these lyrics about that unlucky bowerbird:

> See the bright bird dancing from Papua New Guinea on
> your tv screen?
> He's on a promenade to show the world the fortune he's
> made:
> black beetle's wings and a pile of petals,
> polished stacked and clean, the adornments of the day.
> You want to laugh, but you know this game,
> 'cause you can see his fortune's fate,
> how the skins will wither and colors fade.
> We bargain and we plead with failing currencies,
> but grace is gold for broken banks to hold . . . [3]

We give this hapless bird a nervous laugh because if we look too closely, we might see ourselves, standing center stage among an unappreciated collection of treasures and trophies. What objects define our impressiveness, our worth, or our value—and what do we do when we're told it's simply not enough? Paul had a similar epiphany, with his own dubious collection of blue baubles:

> For it is we who are the circumcision, we who serve God
> by his Spirit, who boast in Christ Jesus, and who put no

> confidence in the flesh—though I myself have reasons for such confidence.
>
> If someone else thinks they have reasons to put confidence in the flesh, I have more: circumcised on the eighth day, of the people of Israel, of the tribe of Benjamin, a Hebrew of Hebrews; in regard to the law, a Pharisee; as for zeal, persecuting the church; as for righteousness based on the law, faultless. (Philippians 3:3–6)

These verses are often referred to as Paul's "Sevenfold Pedigree." If righteousness could be earned, Paul's résumé would hold up against the best contenders. The first four items on his curriculum vitae were status claims. "Circumcised on the eighth day" meant that from the start, his parents did things by the book. "Of the people of Israel" connected Paul to the people of God, not by being grafted in but by birthright. "Of the tribe of Benjamin" cited a family tree that could be traced back to one of the most faithful and favored branches. He sums up his advantaged status with the title "Hebrew of Hebrews."

Having established his status claim, Paul then cites his achievements, leading with "in regard to the law, a Pharisee." Though Jesus's confrontations with the Pharisees of his day have soured this title, in the first century these were the people you wanted as neighbors. They were law-abiding citizens, fastidious in obeying God's commands. "As for zeal, persecuting the church" hearkens back to Paul's pre-conversion exploits as Pharisee Saul, an orthodoxy-pursuing teacher with no qualms about hunting down infidels. Paul concludes with the bold claim, "as for legalistic righteousness, faultless"—not claiming perfection but a meticulous maintenance of the pharisaic interpretation of the law, with all its dietary codes, rituals, and observances. There were no Torah blemishes in his record. Even in his sin, he kept to the sacrificial system. He had enviably clean hands.

But Paul lays all these shiny trophies on his own bower stage and shockingly says, "Whatever were gains to me I now consider loss for the sake of Christ" (3:7). *Loss*? That word in Greek can be translated as "disadvantage." Paul makes the shocking claim that his impressive assortment of assets could actually work *against* him as liabilities. Before meeting Christ, he touted this sevenfold list as his prized identity, his bold grounds of righteousness before the throne. Martin Luther did the same with his status as an earnest Augustinian monk: "I was a good monk, and I kept the rule of my order so strictly that I may say that if ever a monk got to heaven by his monkery it was I."[4] But when Paul and Martin met Jesus, it all got turned upside down.

Our best competencies, when seen as the key components of our identity, become dangerous to us. Their detriment to us lies in our believing, however subtly, that righteousness can be earned. Our lives aren't valuable because we're successful or faithful or funny or religious. Our Sunday School classes may have given us gold stars for good behavior, but heaven's classroom doesn't work that way. In our own self-assessment, we think of our positive qualities—winning personality, steady generosity, good citizenship, you name it—as shiny blue treasures. But what if that treasure is cursed? What if, when we try to grab those things as talismans of our self-definition, they turn on us?

Paul's assessment of his pedigree leaves us with the frightening realization that when we come to Christ, we're not just asked to die to our vices but also our virtues. Paul continues, "I consider them garbage, that I may gain Christ" (3:8). Not just loss, *garbage.* That shocking Greek word—*skubala*—could also be descriptive of dog poop. Dung. Excrement. Paul takes one of the greatest résumés a Jew could possibly assemble and flushes it down the toilet.

A Better Treasure

How could Paul so flippantly throw away the righteous reputation he had worked so hard to achieve? Because he discovered, in Christ, that it wasn't righteousness at all. Everything in Paul's seven bullet points is all about Paul. His perceived pharisaical dignity is a house of cards, incapable of standing before the white-hot holiness of God's throne. He could not build a righteousness that would earn points with the Righteous One. And neither can you. Congratulations.

No, truly: Congratulations! This realization is freedom.

Imagine our luckless bowerbird again. All his hard-fought treasures are displayed upon his self-constructed stage, blue-bejeweled knickknacks that he hopes might catch the eye of approval from a passing female. Females who are open to a serious commitment will commonly visit multiple bowers, circling back to those she finds more promising. She will visit regularly and unannounced, and if our bird is among the finalists, he will have to be always on alert. When the girlfriend might drop in at any moment, you've got to keep the place tidy all the time. This poor bowerbird must keep up appearances, show no weaknesses, withstand her grueling inspections, portray himself as a quality catch that's got it all together. This bird is always onstage, always performing, always living under the microscope.

Have you ever felt that? The pressure to maintain poise? The exhaustion of feeling like you're always on display? The fear of being found out? The anxiety of possible rejection? The certitude that, if people truly knew you, they would turn their backs? Tim Keller was fond of reminding people that every one of us wants to be both known *and* loved; only one or the other simply won't do. To be loved and not known is vapid shallowness; to be known and not loved is aching rejection. The struggle of the bowerbird is a familiar saga for us, doing our dances and arranging our trinkets in a desperate desire to be noticed and maybe even loved.

Paul's self-surrender is a freedom from this exhausting life of performance and posturing. His garbage assessment of his pedigree is not a *loss* as much as it is a *swap,* an identity both lost and found: "that I may gain Christ and be found in him, not having a righteousness of my own that comes from the law, but that which is through faith in Christ—the righteousness that comes from God on the basis of faith" (Philippians 3:8–9). Freedom! This righteousness is not about our performance, our amassed treasure, or our inherent worthiness. It's not about *us* at all, in fact; it's a righteousness that comes from what God has done for us in Christ. If we are incapable of inherent righteousness (true), without which we cannot stand before a holy God (true), our only alternative is for one who is truly righteous to willingly stand in our place. By faith, Jesus does. The Christian is the one who knows Jesus is the *only* credit that counts for righteousness. Paul's loss-and-garbage autobiography is a joyous declaration to his readers: "Please understand, dear Philippians, that before the throne of God my holiest highlight reel will earn me nothing. And neither will yours. But the Righteous One, who earned it all for us, stands in our place. Our hope is found in Christ alone."

One day all our best efforts will be revealed for the cheap blue plastic they are (Isaiah 64:6). But those who stand in the completed righteousness of Jesus will not be met by the hypercritical stare of a derisive lover but by the pursuing gaze of a Savior who paid it all to call us his treasure.

— CHAPTER 11 —

Tern Pursuits

One thing I do: Forgetting what is behind and straining toward what is ahead, I press on toward the goal to win the prize for which God has called me heavenward in Christ Jesus.

—PHILIPPIANS 3:13–14

We human beings are by nature terrestrial, clodhopping creatures. The law of gravity keeps us earth-bound. So we look on the birds with envy. If only we could fly! We sigh longingly with the psalmist: "Oh, that I had the wings of a dove! I would flee far away..." (Psalm 55:8). Flight is to us the symbol of freedom.

—JOHN STOTT[1]

ERWIN MCMANUS WROTE, "There are few things more powerful than a life lived with passionate clarity.... Every moment is waiting to be seized by those who are chasing daylight."[2] The Arctic Tern takes McManus's daylight-chasing challenge very literally. In fact, no animal on the planet does it better.

Each June, large colonies of these birds gather in trendy summer vacation hot spots like Kitsissunnguit, Greenland; Nunavut, Canada; and the island archipelago of Svalbard, five hundred miles north of northernmost Norway. Your travel agent might not recommend these destinations to you, or be able to pronounce them, but the Arctic Tern is passionate for the polar. In these extreme northern latitudes, the Arctic summer sun swings a lazy 360-degree panoramic arc without ever dipping fully below the horizon. The terns bask in twenty-four-hour daylight, their own unconventional interpretation of the Beach Boys' *Endless Summer.*

The Arctic Tern, elegantly streamlined and effortlessly buoyant in air, is crowned with a striking black cap over the head and eyes—a sort of bird rendition of the Dread Pirate Roberts.[3] And like a good pirate, it's seen a fair bit of the world. The earth's tilted axis assures that perpetual light will eventually become a harsh perpetual darkness, so what's a tern to do when the light starts to fade? As summer break transitions to the offseason, they know another great destination that should be open for business soon...

Antarctica.

And so, as the Arctic closes shop for the season, the terns turn their attention southward, hardwired for *the longest migration on the planet.* Their ambitious trip commences with a somber ceremony on a particular day in mid- to late October.

In an abrupt moment, the noisy rookery of 2,500 or more birds will go eerily silent. Their raucous chatter ceases in a coordinated instant—a phenomenon that scientists have termed a "dread." The colony collectively holds its breath, like a silent congregational prayer, a supplication for traveling mercies. Then, out of the reverent hush, the entire flock bursts into the air and circles south, leaving their nests and their silence behind.

No creature on this globe lives more of its life in daylight than the Arctic Tern. That would be true even if the terns made a beeline south. But they don't. Their ninety-day trip meanders in an unhurried path that takes them across four or even five continents. After crossing the North Atlantic, some track south along the coast of Africa, others on the coast of South America. Some do *both,* deciding halfway to cross the ocean again, just for kicks. And a group of solid overachievers will inexplicably round the Cape of Good Hope into the Indian Ocean for a jaunt to Australia. Yes, Australia. That group, let's face it, is just showing off.

Author Scott Weidensaul quips, "Any seabird biologist will admit, especially after a beer or two, that no one really has a clue what the true limits of tern migration might be."[4] Recent studies using geolocator tags have more than doubled the prior predictions of scientists. An ambitious tern, it turns out, might actually travel more than fifty-six thousand miles on their annual commute. Over the twenty- to thirty-year lifespan of the bird, an Arctic Tern will potentially fly *one and a half million miles* in its pursuit of endless summer.

Put that number in perspective. That's over fifty-seven thousand marathons. That's sixty trips around the earth. That's three trips to the moon and back. A friend of mine recently retired from a career that involved extensive international travel. He logged over a million miles of frequent-flier points. I wonder if he ever saw a tern from the window of his plane, flying past with a condescending glance at his platinum-club card.

If the Arctic Tern were to make a New Year's resolution from its January Antarctic roost, perhaps it would sound something like this: *I will do whatever it takes to live as fully in the light as this little globe allows me to.*

Now It's Your Tern

An Arctic Tern would already make a fitting mascot for a globe-trotting missionary like the apostle Paul, who logged some serious miles on his migrations through the Mediterranean. But Paul's pursuit wasn't ultimately about the frequent-flier miles; he had a more significant goal in mind—one that could still be pursued from a prison cell. Notwithstanding his chains, Paul describes the journey before him as a marathon,

> Not that I have already obtained all this, or have already arrived at my goal, but I press on to take hold of that for which Christ Jesus took hold of me. Brothers and sisters, I do not consider myself yet to have taken hold of it. But one thing I do: Forgetting what is behind and straining toward what is ahead, I press on toward the goal to win the prize for which God has called me heavenward in Christ Jesus. (Philippians 3:12–14)

The Arctic Tern is truly the king of "pressing on toward the goal"—living as a lover of the light, keeping the sun ever before him. In these verses, Paul describes a similar pursuit, orienting toward the light and fixing his horizon on the purposes of Jesus—keeping the *Son* ever before him. It's his response to grace, "[taking] hold of that for which Christ Jesus took hold of me." After all, why did Jesus take hold of Paul? Why does he take hold of *you*? Jesus's grip is more than a fast pass to heaven: It's an invitation to grip back. It's a commitment to aim our wings where the light may be found. First John 1:5 says: "God is light; in him there is no darkness at all." And so if God is light, dear reader, then may you be an Arctic Tern. May you live so fully in the light that it *defines* you. May every wingbeat of your journey be a quest for Son-shine.

And yet, let's face it, those words are pretty vague. Inspiring, maybe, but generic—because really, what does it *mean* to live in the light? If we're going to build our lives around this goal, we need more specificity. So, before you get that tern tattoo, let's consider three answers to that question—each of which might fall short if taken alone: pursuing *righteousness,* pursuing *honesty,* and pursuing *gospel.*

Pursuing Righteousness

Psalm 97:11 says, "Light shines on the righteous and joy on the upright in heart." The pursuit of righteousness is a determined commitment to live in the light. It's living before the face of God—*coram Deo*—aligning our actions with his radiance, his will with ours. Our daily pursuit of God's glory bears compound interest over time: "The path of the righteous is like the morning sun, shining ever brighter till the full light of day" (Proverbs 4:18). Do rightly and you will see his light.

And yet my greatest obstacle to a light-filled life is more formidable than any ocean or polar ice. My greatest obstacle to living in the light is . . . me.

You don't need a Bible verse or a counseling degree to know this is true of you. Just recount the last time someone confronted you with an aspect of your character that was too true to deny but too painful to own. Faithful are the wounds of a friend. And yet, rather than embrace the blade, it's more likely that the shame of the moment transports us back to a tarnished garden, a place where the cool-of-the-day radiance of God triggered a compulsive desire to hide. "I was afraid because I was naked; so I hid" (Genesis 3:10). Light creates shame. Shame creates fear. Fear creates hiding. When faced with an aspect of ourselves that can't abide the light, we grab the fig leaves. We scurry like insects back under the rotten log of our secretive safety. The darkness feels safe, yes, but it is death to us.

The pursuit of holiness is a pursuit of light. And yet by itself, this pursuit will only leave us discouraged in our failures or smug in our successes. It's sobering to remember that the uber-righteous Pharisee Nicodemus—a man committed to a lifetime of purity—came to Jesus under cover of darkness, asking his questions in shadow, hiding for fear that his messianic interests would sabotage his religious reputation. Jesus told him, "This is the verdict: Light has come into the world, but people loved darkness instead of light because their deeds were evil" (John 3:19). His words beckon Nicodemus, and us, to pursue a light that is more than moral purity.

Pursuing Honesty

Living in the light also means living honestly with respect to our darkness. This involves an honest-to-God acknowledgment of our rebellion and resistance but also an honest-to-others authenticity. The apostle John follows that "God is light" verse with this one: "If we walk in the light, as he is in the light, we have fellowship *with one another*" (1 John 1:7). Isn't that a surprising turn? Wouldn't you expect him to finish that sentence with "fellowship with *God*"? Instead we get the encouragement that pursuing light empowers fellowship with each other. Darkness enables facade, but light enables relationship.

Dane Ortlund, in his book *Deeper: Real Change for Real Sinners,* describes the outcomes of this authenticity:

> In the darkness, your sins fester and grow in strength. In the light, they wither and die. Walking in the light, in other words, is honesty with God and others....
>
> We consign ourselves to plateaued growth in Christ if we yield to pride and fear and hide our sins. We grow as we own up to being real sinners, not theoretical sinners. All of us, as Christians, acknowledge generally that we are sinners. Rarer is the Christian who opens up to another about exactly *how* he or she is a sinner. But in this honesty, life blossoms.[5]

Living in the light requires risky transparency. The shadows may be more flattering—like dark photo filters that mask the imperfections—but they're deceiving. Light indeed reveals our unsightliness, but light also frees us from the prison of pretending.

And yet this second concept of light-living, like the first, falls short by itself. Without one additional step, a commitment to honesty will only leave us with the platitudes of "Nobody's perfect" or "This is just who I am, so deal with it." It enables the sort of accountability group that answers one another's confessions with "Try harder next week." Honesty about our failures gives us permission to admit where we're sick but doesn't offer a cure. We may be able to tell the receptionist at the doctor's office where it hurts, but she can't write our prescription.

Pursuing Gospel

For the Christian, walking in hope necessitates a third sort of light-living. It's more than a commitment to righteousness or honesty, as important as those commitments are. It's a commitment to the person and the work of Jesus himself: "I am the light of the world. Whoever follows me will never walk in darkness, but will have the light of life" (John 8:12). Light is embodied in Jesus, the one who gifts us with a forgiveness that removes the sting of death and an honesty that removes the barb of shame.

As a pastor, I can think of two instances when a visiting couple has told me after the Sunday service, in words this direct, "We're good people looking for a good church full of good people, and we like it here because you seem like good people." Both times I've given the same answer. It begins with an honest laugh, followed by "Boy, are we going to disappoint you. Because we're not good people." A brief awkward silence follows, after which I say, "We're not good people, but we're forgiven people, and if you stick around here long enough, I believe you'll come to discover the difference." Both couples stayed, and over time became dear family to us. More than that, both couples *did* come to discover the difference, declare their need, embrace Jesus, and become beautiful trophies of his grace.

Good people may not be the same as forgiven people, but aren't forgiven people joyously motivated to live as good people? I'm convinced that's what Paul is saying in Philippians 3:16, one of the most perfectly concise wow moments of the whole letter: "Only let us live up to what we have already attained." Ponder those words for a moment. What have we already attained? We've been declared *righteous.* Spotless. Holy. That declaration doesn't come from our pedigree, performance, or proficiency, as we saw in the last chapter. It's an "alien righteousness" that's entirely outside of us—found not in *our* work on God's behalf but in *God's* work on ours. Paul's claim to goodness is "not having a righteousness of my own that comes from the law, but that which is through faith in Christ—the righteousness that comes from God on the basis of faith" (3:9).

What does that reality do to your heart? I suppose you can take it as a free pass—some sort of permission to put your sanctification on cruise control. Or, like Paul, it can propel you to fly to the poles and back again in grateful response. Put simply, by faith you are *already* defined by the light of his holiness. This is how God sees you: not an enemy shivering in the polar darkness but a child of the light. "For you were once darkness, but now you are light in the Lord" (Ephesians 5:8). Now *go live like it.*

Guaranteed, we will have dark moments on the journey, with our sin on full display. We will have a bad moment, a hard day, an unfortunate outburst, or a colossal belly flop into our own dark capacities. In that moment, we may lament that we're not living in the light and tuck those misdeeds away in the shadows, hoping others won't see or will soon forget. There may be some repentance in that, but gospel light is so much more. It is *freedom.* It's not just admitting our wrongs but reveling in the forgiveness we have in the light of Christ, claiming the gospel's realities, and seeing grace change us.

Live up to what you have *already* attained. So by all means, live in the light of righteousness, determined to glorify God with your life. And live in the light of honesty, free to admit where you regularly fall short of his glory. But most of all, live in the light of the gospel, the good news that frees us *from* shame and *to* the pursuit of holiness. May yours be a pole-to-pole commitment to the gospel, allowing its radical promises to wow you. Jesus entered the judgment of polar darkness to give you the hope of perpetual light. Keep telling yourself the good news, and let others speak it to you regularly, until the day when Christ becomes so fully our light that no migration will be necessary: "Night will be no more. They will need no light of lamp or sun, for the Lord God will be their light" (Revelation 22:5, ESV).

— CHAPTER 12 —

The Homing of Pigeons

Our citizenship is in heaven. And we eagerly await a Savior from there, the Lord Jesus Christ, who, by the power that enables him to bring everything under his control, will transform our lowly bodies so that they will be like his glorious body.

—PHILIPPIANS 3:20–21

"Your true nesting place lies farther on."

"Lies where?" I asked.

He said, "Godric, this much at least I know for sure. Until you reach it, every other place you find will fret you like a cage."

—FREDERICK BUECHNER[1]

THERE WAS A cage next to the casket.

As a pastor, I've officiated plenty of funerals and graveside services, but this odd item was a first for me. As family and friends in their somber colors processed from their line of cars to the graveside tent, I asked the funeral home director what the deal was with the cage. He confided that this was a special service provided for families upon request. He spoke these words with a funeral-whisper somberness, but I could definitely tell he was excited about it.

The cage was wire, the dimensions of a largish mailbox, and covered with a cloth. Inside, something was *moving.* My imagination (and my seminary training) didn't have a category for this. Did someone bring this poor woman's *cat* to the funeral?

After my short readings, pronouncements, and prayer, the director escorted the mourners from the funeral tent onto the open lawn and began a carefully memorized script delivered in a genteel Southern accent. As a symbol of "our dearly departed arriving safely into the arms of heaven, having slipped the surly bonds of earth," three white doves would be released as a representation of the Father, Son, and Holy Spirit, followed by a fourth dove rising to meet them, a picture of the departed "newly freed from the bondage of this world and now seeking her way to eternal glory." The script continued: "And behold, ye family and friends, as this Trinitarian flock meets the freed soul in the air to guide our loved one to her heavenly home."

You might think that, as both a birder and a pastor, I was excited by this symbolic ceremony. Instead, if I'm honest, my inner theologian rolled his eyes. Aside from the Trinitarian misrepresentations (only the Holy Spirit gets dove status, right?) and the Plato-inspired body-as-the-prison-of-the-soul motif, the whole moment felt heavy on the cheese factor. But I stood respectfully. At least it wasn't a cat.

As classical music swelled from a portable speaker, the three doves launched high in unison and took up a wide circling formation, maybe fifty feet above us. Then, after another scripted sentence naming the deceased, the director released the fourth bird. It rose in a purposeful flutter of white feathers and joined the orbit, quickly closing the distance with the others. The four birds merged into one flight path, circling once more as the music swelled on cue. And then they were gone, turning due south and disappearing over the treetops.

I found myself genuinely clapping along with the crowd, even brushing back an uninvited tear. It was moving, cheese notwithstanding. After the ceremony, I peppered the director with questions. How do you train three birds to circle a cemetery? How do they know to wait for the fourth bird? How many bird quartets have you released into the wild to fend for themselves? Has a stray hawk ever "stolen the show"?

I was thankful to learn that these doves were actually homing pigeons, not abandoned to the woods but rather homeward bound, flying back to their roost about thirty miles south across the state line. When released, they naturally circle the area in order to get their bearings, engaging their inner GPS. After a few laps, their brain locks in their destination with absolute precision. They're home in time for dinner, ready for the next ceremony.

The pigeon performance was a unique ceremony to be sure, but it represents an all-too-common human instinct. At a funeral we often fumble to get our bearings as we stand between two worlds, grabbing for words and metaphors to make sense of the wrongness of the moment. We were made to *live;* our hearts feel this certainty because the Lord has written eternity into them (Ecclesiastes 3:11). That hardwiring also gives us a strange sense of homelessness here. Have you felt it?

Paul's exhortation to the Philippians helps us process this tug we feel—made for here, yet made for more—and does so through the concept of *citizenship:* "Our citizenship is in heaven. And we eagerly await a Savior from there, the Lord Jesus Christ, who, by the power that enables him to bring everything under his control, will transform our lowly bodies so that they will be like his glorious body" (Philippians 3:20–21). Those words give us something to live out and something to look toward, and the lowly pigeon offers inspiration for both: earthly purposefulness and heavenly bearings.

The Pigeon's Fall from Grace

That unconventional graveside service may have been my first encounter with a homing pigeon, but humans have harnessed the power of this bird for at least five thousand years. "Wherever civilization has flourished, there the pigeon has thrived, and the higher the civilization, usually the higher the regard for the pigeon." If you think that quote sounds like it was written by someone with an overinflated view of pigeons, you're probably right; Wendell Mitchell Levi was the first lieutenant in charge of the pigeon brigade for the U.S. Army Signal Corps in World War I. Yes, our armed forces had a pigeon brigade. In fact, so did the Germans. And not to be outdone, the British had both a pigeon unit and an anti-pigeon unit—Peregrine Falcons that were trained to intercept German birds (a colossal failure, since the falcons only intercepted seven pigeons with messages, and they were all British).[2]

Pigeons in both world wars were given medals for key missions, and some of them figured prominently into the outcome of battles, like the famous bird Cher Ami, who saved 194 soldiers—the Lost Battalion—in the Argonne in 1918 by successfully delivering this message to high command: "We are along the road paralell [*sic*] 276.4. Our own artillery is dropping a barrage directly on us. For heavens sake stop it." Cher Ami took a German bullet and lost a leg but received the Croix de Guerre medal for his mission and gained such fame that today his stuffed one-legged body sits atop a perch in the Smithsonian National Museum of American History. Author Kathleen Rooney imagines what sort of motivational *carpe diem* exhortation Cher Ami might whisper to us today: "Monuments matter most to pigeons and soldiers.... In life I was both a pigeon and a soldier. In death I am a piece of mediocre taxidermy, collecting dust."[3] Seize the day, boys.

We've known for some time, apparently, that pigeons get the job done. In the fifth century B.C., a communication line of pigeon couriers connected the cities of Persia and Syria. In ancient Rome, results of the Olympics were publicized by pigeon. And names familiar to us today for keeping the world quickly informed—Reuters for breaking news and Rothschild for financial updates—owe their start-up strategy to the pigeon.[4]

But it's safe to say that, in most circles, this noble résumé has been forgotten. Many birders might not even think to count *Columba livia* as a bird on their life lists. Perhaps it's because they're so common—over four hundred million worldwide, and growing with increased urbanization. Perhaps it's because they're so adapted to city dwelling that they seem more like part of the architectural world than the natural one. Perhaps it's the billions of dollars a year that we spend cleaning up their poop (and restoring the damage caused by it). Yes, the noble pigeon's reputation has been tarnished. Sure, we're fine with *doves,* but we don't name milk chocolate or white bar soap after pigeons, nor do we refer to the event at the baptism of Jesus as "the Spirit coming down from heaven as a pigeon." We've even formally severed the family relationship; in 2003 the American Ornithologists' Union officially changed the common name of *Columba livia* from Rock Dove to Rock Pigeon. When your family votes to change your last name, they might be trying to tell you something.

Of all the glorious birds on our planet, I can't believe I'm dedicating a whole chapter to *this* one (and the next chapter, for that matter, to the equally maligned House Sparrow), but I've realized that pigeons deserve some respect. In fact, the next time you hear that telltale *coo* in your local park, remember that human history has relied significantly on the little brain under that vacant stare. Metaphorically speaking, we've put a lot of eggs in that basket. That odd gray-and-iridescent creature mooching your breadcrumbs may have a more accurate sense of direction than your smartphone. It knows exactly where it is and exactly where it's going, embodying both an uncanny sense of the moment and a grounded anticipation of home. Don't we need a better capacity for both, knowing what it means to live *here* as citizens of *there*?

Oriented for Home

When Paul writes that "our citizenship is in heaven," he's reminding his readers of that Ecclesiastes sense of eternity that's already stamped on their hearts. We often repress this sense, chalking it up to wishful thinking or the practicality of the now. But repressed or not, we have an innate sense of direction for another world, born from God's blueprint as his image bearers and manifested in the persistent itch that this world is unfinished, awaiting final restoration, an egg waiting to hatch. C. S. Lewis wrote, "If I find in myself a desire which no experience in this world can satisfy, the most probable explanation is that I was made for another world."[5] If you've ever felt the disappointment of a world that doesn't seem to work the way it should—or the heart in your own chest that doesn't work the way *it* should—you know what I'm talking about. The pains we witness, and the pains we ourselves inflict (intentional or not), create a tug on our hearts for justice, fairness, harmony, peace, rest, joy, and perfect love. That stirring we feel is a holy discontent, and we realize in those moments that home is calling. We have a sense of what the recipe should look like, but we keep checking the oven, and it's clearly not done yet. So we wait, hungry but hopeful, anticipating the moment when all the ingredients finally blend into the glorious meal they were made for.

Paul affirms that longing. Yes, he says, this world is a disaster, but not forever. The world is full of people fighting for scraps in a society that's focused on lesser things (Philippians 3:18). But you, Philippian Christians, lift your heads up, look higher, and fix your eyes on the One who will perfect your faith (Hebrews 12:2). Our earnest hope is a transformed creation and a transformed people, and we "eagerly await a Savior" who will bring these things to pass (Philippians 3:20–21). The Christian life is a life of longing, a glorious anticipation of all things made new, all under the powerful control of the most benevolent King. To understand who you truly are, lock in on those heavenly coordinates; let them be your true north.

Imagine if someone dropped you blindfolded in a cornfield somewhere in the middle of Nebraska, telling you to find your way back home. No, you can't use your iPhone. No, you can't consult the road signs on the interstate or even one of those old AAA TripTiks or truck-stop maps. Suddenly that pigeon doesn't look so ditzy, does it? Its sense of home is so hardwired that wherever you drop it on the map, it just takes a couple of circles in the air to lock in the coordinates to its hometown.

Plenty of birds have this harnessed capacity of map and compass, allowing for the remarkable phenomenon of migration. Those Scarlet Tanagers that nested in your yard this summer are likely the same ones who nested in your yard last summer, after spending the winter at their *casita* in central Peru. How birds do this is an ongoing mystery. "I find it oddly thrilling that the mental maps of birds remain . . . well . . . unmapped," says Jennifer Ackerman in *The Genius of Birds*. "There's no clear evidence that any one sensory cue is the whole story."[6] All we've managed to determine is that it's partially learned, partially innate, partially the earth's magnetism, partially the spin of the stars, partially the angle of the sun, partially sight, possibly infrasound, and possibly even smell. Think of an airplane's dashboard. We know that some gauges are more useful for laying a flight path, and others kick in for navigating at lower altitudes or closer to the final destination. But all of those add together to provide both a fine-tuned compass and an astonishing spatial map. Like Disney's *Moana* family sings, "When it's time to find home, we know the way."[7]

From wherever we are on the map, from whatever moment we inhabit, we function best when our soul's final destination is locked in. Our destination defines us. As author Dennis Johnson writes, "The city that defines your identity is neither the one in which you were born nor the one in which you were raised. It is the city toward which you are moving."[8]

Heaven on Earth

Heaven. That's where we're going. But what does that mean for us tomorrow morning? This heavenly hope also has to be strong enough to ground our current circumstances with purpose, shaking off that nagging feeling of homelessness and focusing us on living intentionally now. After all, everything in our lives (not just our final destination) is shaped by what kingdom we think we're citizens of.

The word *citizenship* in Philippians 3:20 isn't just an identity; it's a mission—and one the Philippians understood better than most. Philippi was declared a Roman colony to celebrate the famous battle waged there. After Julius Caesar's assassination by his senate, his loyal generals Mark Antony and Octavian pursued and defeated the assassins Brutus and Cassius at the Battle of Philippi in 42 B.C. To commemorate the vindication of the Republic, Philippi was declared a Roman colony, and all its eligible inhabitants were granted the privilege of Roman citizenship.

To be a citizen of Rome, for the Philippians, didn't mean they were *from* Rome or that they needed to move *to* Rome. Instead, they lived in Philippi as representatives of a different city. They were proud of their Roman citizenship, and when Paul pointed their true citizenship heavenward, he was giving their reality a wider context. They'd already been representing a kingdom that they hadn't seen yet. Now they were charged with representing a nobler one.

Too often we think of our eternal home with an escapist mentality. We want to go to heaven for the same reason we want to go to Hawaii: We've heard it's a nice place and we could use the rest. But if we are already citizens of heaven, as followers of Christ, our future hope has present implications. We're not just called to escape from this world to that one; we're called to bring *that* one into *this* one. We live to manifest a partial answer to that astounding three-word prayer, "Thy kingdom come." The goal isn't just to get back to the coop; we have a message to deliver.

This grounds us. It gives us wings but also feet—ground to claim for the realities of God's kingdom. We get the privilege to speak the realities of heaven into the atmosphere of earth. We bring the language of our passport country into the borders of our host country.

Knowing Your Place

What's your post in the kingdom? In God's sovereign plan, you've been stationed for a purpose. Consider your place for a moment: real GPS coordinates in a real neighborhood under real clouds. It's increasingly hard for us to live within the context of real space and time. Today we can post a comment online that is simultaneously everywhere and nowhere at all. We know our screens better than we know the weather outside. Our broad digital reach becomes the strangely undefined space in which we "live and move and have our being" (Acts 17:28). Locality feels limiting to us. To borrow from Zack Eswine, we "strive to be everywhere at once. But to be everywhere generally is to reside nowhere particularly. To strive for various things at once is to announce one's secession from place."[9] Yes, we want to bring heavenly realities to bear on our earthly calling, but first we need a sticker on our map that says, "You are here."

There are those who excel in living within the geographic specificity of place: Thoreau at Walden Pond, Annie Dillard at Tinker Creek, Jayber Crow in Port William. Few of us possess that level of reflective attentiveness. But while it would be great to know the names of the trees in your yard or the seasonal arrivals of monarchs or warblers, I intend something more than that. Your purpose includes your place. God has sovereignly set you on the map, in *this* place and time.

Consider this: Jesus had a hometown. He was known as Jesus *of Nazareth*, a Savior with a zip code. His cosmic work was rooted in the dusty roads of his childhood town (and later Capernaum). He had family there and provided a local woodworking service to the community. He knew the folks four miles up the road in Cana well enough to drop in on a wedding (John 2:1–5). The Holy One from heaven walked the paths of Nazareth, breathed its air, pulled water from the town well, and knew the local fishing holes. In a town with fewer than four thousand residents, he greeted his neighbors by name and knew their stories. Andrew Peterson adds, "Jesus . . . had time to spot the wildflowers, converse with his friends, and experience a culture built to human (and not automobile) scale. He lived his life at three miles per hour."[10] The One through whom all things were made (Colossians 1:16) humbled himself to live locally, to call a remote first-century village *home.*

"Rabbi, where are you from?"

"Well, the eternal throne room of God but, more recently, 123 Main Street, Nazareth."

I remember driving to the local high school for my weekly visit years ago as a youth pastor in Georgia. Shortcutting down a country road through cornfields, it hit me in a purpose-defining moment that a sovereign, holy God had called me to participate in his global kingdom plan in this local rural-suburban county, population twenty-four thousand. This was my post. This was my precise place to make the invisible kingdom visible. My big-picture, seminary-equipped vision for transforming the whole world suddenly felt as wonderfully grounded as that cornfield. Far from confining, that moment gifted me with the freedom of roots.

God may change our kingdom post, and he often does. Others have since taken up my old role in that wonderful Georgia county. In a line that has followed me securely through several moves and potential moves, Rich Mullins sings, "I am home anywhere if you are where I am."[11] But here's what you can know for certain today...

You. Are. Here.

God has geography-specific intentions for you today, right where you are. Owning that, to quote Eswine, "may simply require you to stop trying to get somewhere other than where you already are."[12] Maybe that means you can name the trees in your yard or the birds in your feeder. But how much better if you can name the neighbors on your street? When Jesus said to "love your neighbor," his definition included those well beyond the borders of a cul-de-sac (Luke 10:27–37), but shouldn't it start there? When we define our neighbor as anyone, does the vagueness of that definition allow us to look right past the person next door? As Rick Rusaw and Brian Mavis explain in their book *The Neighboring Church,* "We don't just love the neighbors we choose but the ones God chooses for us."[13] To think intentionally about your current locality, start by considering the five households closest to your doorstep. Do you know the names of the people who live there? How about their backstories? Recent defining moments? Heaviest concerns? Why not make a goal of filling in some of those blanks, even this week? A care for locality is a care for *people.* It's the second-greatest commandment, and you have a home address from which to live it out.

A New Hometown

I will never have a pigeon's acuity for home, to be able to discern the smell and magnetism of a place and distinguish it from other spots on the map. I can't even remember where I parked my car at the mall. But I *can* be a student of the place God has sovereignly put me, to know its beauty and brokenness, its niceties and needs, the stories it tells. And I can do so as a citizen of heaven, representing the realities of a different city. These two destinations—being fully present here and fully ready for there—aren't competing flight paths but a single trajectory that seeks the glory of God. C. S. Lewis wrote, "If you read history you will find that the Christians who did most for the present world were just those who thought most of the next."[14]

One day our souls—by faith in the hometown Nazarene—will circle three laps of the cemetery and fix our wings on a course not yet traveled yet strangely familiar. From there, we'll await a bodily resurrection in a new hometown. Until then, may the Lord find us faithful as kingdom citizens.

— CHAPTER 13 —

Considering Sparrows

Do not be anxious about anything, but in every situation, by prayer and petition, with thanksgiving, present your requests to God. And the peace of God, which transcends all understanding, will guard your hearts and your minds in Christ Jesus.

—PHILIPPIANS 4:6–7

You see, he is making the birds our schoolmasters and teachers. It is a great and abiding disgrace to us that in the Gospel a helpless sparrow should become a theologian and a preacher to the wisest of men. We have as many teachers and preachers as there are little birds in the air.

—MARTIN LUTHER[1]

ROUGHLY ESTIMATED, THERE'S one House Sparrow on this planet for every five humans. This ratio is reversed at outdoor bagel shops.

A 2021 study estimated the world's House Sparrow population to be over 1.6 billion, making it the most numerous wild bird in existence.[2] Anywhere you find humans, you're apt to find a House Sparrow: They're that funny little brown bird with the black bib that mooches your breadcrumbs at Firehouse Subs, flits noisily through the rafters in the garden section at Home Depot, or makes a nest out of that hole in your vinyl siding (you really should get that fixed, you know). They're the bird you see when you aren't even birdwatching—unbelievably common and ridiculously adapted to human settlement. And for at least the last eleven thousand years, since the dawn of agriculture, that's where they've lived almost exclusively.

When Jesus told his disciples to consider the birds (Matthew 6:26), there's a good chance that he was referring to a House Sparrow. Odds are also good that, up to that point, no one listening to Jesus's sermon had bothered to consider said sparrow, except possibly as a chirpy nuisance—the vermin on the mount. If Jesus's intention was to pick an object devoid of perceived value, he couldn't have found a better example. Why? Because in the span of human history, despite the House Sparrow's obvious desire to cozy up to humans, the feeling has not been reciprocated.

The Devaluation of Sparrows

Consult your field guide for a description of a House Sparrow and you'll find unflattering words like *drab, plain, dingy,* and *dull*—words that Sherwin-Williams is unlikely to use in naming their next line of semi-gloss paints. Perhaps the most scathing insult is found in my guide to the birds of Southeast Asia; it writes off the House Sparrow with the word "nondescript." Even people who make a *living* writing about birds find this specimen uninteresting, indistinct, forgettable.

Beyond simply labeling the House Sparrow unremarkable, many find this bird to be outright *offensive.* The eighteenth-century French naturalist Georges-Louis Leclerc, Comte de Buffon, makes no effort to disguise his contempt: "It is extremely destructive, its plumage is entirely useless, its flesh is indifferent food, its notes are grating to the ear, and its familiarity and petulance are disgusting."[3] I'm sure Buffon was a fun guy to go birdwatching with. Frankly though, his indictment matches the public attitude throughout history, both in its native Eurasia and the other four continents where the bird has been introduced.

Consider the bird's immigration to the shores of America, for instance. It's believed that the New World's first House Sparrows were released in New York City by Nicolas Pike of the Brooklyn Institute in 1850. Eight pairs were released, a move that surely ranks highly on history's "But Really, What Could Go Wrong?" list. Despite "a few protests from intelligent naturalists who opposed its introduction" and "a few warnings from naturalized citizens who had spent many years fighting the bird in their native land,"[4] the public largely found the birds charming and believed they would help curb a nagging inchworm infestation. Successive releases occurred over the next two decades: twenty in Boston Common; eighty in New Haven, Connecticut; two hundred more in New York City; and in 1869 a whopping one thousand birds in Philadelphia. This, dear reader, is how a revolution begins—but it's also the recipe for a pandemic.

Just thirty years later, the U.S. Department of Agriculture

released a four-hundred-page report chronicling the havoc wreaked by these European interlopers, both as public nuisances in the city and as crop destroyers in the country. "It is impossible to mark the precise date at which the tide of public opinion turned against the Sparrow," wrote the author of the report, Walter Barrows.[5] But turn it did. In some states bounties were offered—a penny for every dead bird—and the war was on. Now deemed a menace to society, the birds were demonized with language that mirrored the era's unkind sentiment toward European and Chinese immigrants. The House Sparrow was portrayed as "a foreigner . . . that competes unfairly with native birds, . . . that has an immoral character, and . . . that needs to be eliminated from the American community of birds."[6] Even a children's book about birds dubbed House Sparrows "bad citizens and criminals" in a scathing judgment: "This disreputable tramp not only does no work for his taxes—he hates honest work, like all vagrants—but . . . drives away the industrious native birds who are good Citizens. . . . He is a very bad bird, who ought to suffer the extreme penalty of the law."[7] Wait, we're still talking about *birds,* right? The sparrow discussion became a nationalistic metaphor and a veiled threat. It was not a good era of history to be an immigrant, either human or bird.

In other epicenters of sparrow invasion, the response has been similar. Mao Tse-tung *literally* declared war on the closely related Eurasian Tree Sparrow in 1958 during the Great Leap Forward campaign, deeming it one of the four pests that posed a clear and present danger to a flourishing Chinese culture. The propaganda against the sparrow (along with the rat, mosquito, and fly) included posters of valiantly posed children brandishing slingshots and wearing sashes of dead birds over their shoulders. The posters bore the slogan: "Everyone come to fight sparrows." And they did. On day one of the campaign, over three million citizens assembled predawn in the streets of Peking with bugles, whistles, cymbals, pots, and pans. At the signal, the city erupted in a cacophony intended to exhaust and scare the sparrows to death. The citizen army marched, yelled, banged, and sang, "Arise, arise, Oh millions with one heart; braving the enemy's fire, march on." Three hundred ten thousand "enemy" birds died in the Peking streets—over four million in the rest of China.[8]

In retrospect, Chairman Mao overplayed his hand. Chinese scientists discovered too late that these sparrows ate insects, not just grain. The rapid decrease in insect-eating birds meant a rapid increase in crop-eating insects. Though Mao believed the sparrow was a threat to crop production and that grain yields would boom with their eradication, the subsequent rise in locusts and other insects had the exact opposite effect and contributed to the Great Chinese Famine the next year that killed over thirty million people. A tragic case of nature's revenge: "My people are destroyed from lack of knowledge" (Hosea 4:6).

The Chinese government modified the campaign quickly, replacing the fourth pest with the bedbug—to the disappointment of slingshot-wielding children everywhere.[9]

Setting the Bar Low

Despite our ages-long battle against this particular species, we can reasonably estimate that three out of every hundred individual wild birds on this planet today are House Sparrows.[10] They've prospered among the centers of humanity, living where we live and thriving where we thrive. Unlike more reclusive species, they opt for the urban. As David Allen Sibley summarizes, "The House Sparrow is one of the most successful and adaptable birds in the world."[11] Maybe they simply enjoy being around us. But as I said, the feeling has not been mutual. Perhaps familiarity breeds contempt.

With that in mind, it's unsettling that when Jesus says "consider the birds," he's potentially talking about a House Sparrow. "Look at the birds of the air; they do not sow or reap or store away in barns, and yet your heavenly Father feeds them. Are you not much more valuable than they? Can any one of you by worrying add a single hour to your life?" (Matthew 6:26–27). Jesus is using a lesser example to prove a greater one, a Jewish technique called a *kal va-homer* ("light and heavy") argument: "If *x* is true, how much more so is *y* true." Where you start in that comparison says something about where you're going. Jesus could have started with a more respectable or beloved bird (in Luke 12:24, in the same argument, he points to the raven—a bird of more reasonable capacities). Imagine Jesus starting with "Consider the Golden Eagle" or "Consider the Resplendent Quetzal." A listener would think, "Now *there's* a place I can build from." If God's promise to us is greater than or equal to *x,* let's hope that *x* is a decent promise already, right?

Instead, Jesus directs our gaze to the lowest rung on the ladder, a dusty brown annoyance that my grandmother simply called a *sputzie* because it wasn't worthy of a more specific ID. Must we start *here,* Lord? If you want us to understand our dignity in the sight of God, why direct us to the most easily overlooked—and even disdained—aspects of your creation?

The same comparison, more species-specific, is on display a few chapters later in Matthew 10:29, where Jesus asks, "Are not two sparrows sold for a penny?" (In the parallel passage of Luke 12:6, Jesus may have found a buy-four-get-one-free coupon: "Are not five sparrows sold for two pennies?") Once again, that trifling price tag is hardly an honorable comparison, and yet the low-valued sparrow appears as Jesus's foundational argument for an anxiety-free life.

That's exactly the point though. What humans overlook, the Father sees. He values even the things we devalue, and he does so with intimate deliberateness. Jesus uses all these questions of avian value to solidify the truth of God's compassion, "Yet not one of them will fall to the ground outside your Father's care." A sovereign God cares—truly cares—about the falling of a sparrow. Imagine that. On a sparrow's final day, God cares about it, counts its feathers, knows the moment of its last breath, and prepares the exact spot of ground that receives its fall. In this simple reassurance from Jesus, God's sovereign compassion is staggering.

Jesus leverages this truth to reassure us of the Father's care for his children: "Therefore I tell you, do not worry about your life" (Matthew 6:25); "do not worry about tomorrow, for tomorrow will worry about itself" (6:34); "don't be afraid; you are worth more than many sparrows" (10:31). What elevates our confidence in his care is not man's view of sparrows (which isn't much) but God's. God takes time for sparrows. *Kal vahomer!* How much more does he providentially love his children?

Anxious for Nothing

Jesus's birdwatching is the reason Paul can write these well-known words to the Philippians, "Do not be anxious about anything, but in every situation, by prayer and petition, with thanksgiving, present your requests to God. And the peace of God, which transcends all understanding, will guard your hearts and your minds in Christ Jesus" (Philippians 4:6–7). Those words have gotten a lot of God's people through a lot of hardship, and I'm guessing you can relate. There have been times in my own life—like when the police are at the door, or when the doctor is ordering further tests—when fear was so gripping that the only thing I could manage to pray was this passage, repeated over and over until it started to stick. Those panicked, lonely places can be met with the confidence that "His eye is on the sparrow, and I know He watches me."[12]

The most-often-repeated command in the Bible is "Fear not!" God has to repeat that encouragement to humanity from Abraham (Genesis 15:1) all the way to Revelation (Revelation 2:10), which says a lot about our propensity for anxiety. Paul's encouragement in Philippians 4 to let go of anxiety isn't a heartless command to "just stop it" but an exercise rooted in thankful reflection. He appeals to us to reflect on God's goodness in order to resist our anxiety triggers. We pray with *thanksgiving,* not despair. We recall the places God has demonstrated his faithful presence and care, prodding our hearts to remember and rejoice. Think of gratitude as a personal trophy case of undeniable God moments, each one ready to be pulled out when the need for calming perspective arises.

"This one is where he showed up after a painful breakup."
"This one was that unexpected check that miraculously allowed us to replace our car."
"This one was when he surprised us all and healed my son."

Those are some of mine. I'm sure you have amazing-grace trophies in your own case as well that have the uncanny capacity to calm your panicked heart. When was the last time you pulled them out, rehearsed God's faithfulness, and gave thanks?

Those trophy-case-of-grace moments give us confidence that he'll be faithful when we face the unknown. If you've experienced that perspective swap, you know what comes next. *Peace.* A peace "which transcends all understanding." I wish I could explain it, but it does, after all, transcend understanding. It lightens our souls and unburdens our hearts. It doesn't alleviate the situation, but it neutralizes our fear of it. Take heart: You are worth more than many sparrows.

In your trophy case of God's faithfulness, keep this one front and center, "He who did not spare his own Son, but gave him up for us all—how will he not also, along with him, graciously give us all things?" (Romans 8:32). If you struggle to see God's goodness in the short span of your life, simply rewind two thousand years. We who have every reason to shrink from God's presence have been brought near by the Cross of Christ. We who have no warrant to approach a holy throne have been presented righteous by faith. When you "present your requests with thanksgiving" and recount the tales of his demonstrated provision, lead your list with praise for the sacrificial love of your Savior. Far greater than the seed of sparrows and the clothing of lilies (Matthew 6:28–29), Jesus feeds us with the bread of life and clothes us in his own righteousness. The reason Paul could say, a few verses later, "My God will meet all your needs according to the riches of his glory in Christ Jesus" (Philippians 4:19) is because *God already had.* The Cross is the down payment on every other answered prayer.

In a particularly distressing season of Joni Eareckson Tada's battle with quadriplegia and chronic pain, her husband Ken hung a bird feeder outside her window, an attempt to bring some joy and beauty to an anxious moment. When the sparrows found it, Joni was reminded of the bird promises of our Savior:

> I glanced at the bird feeder and smiled. I could understand Jesus noticing an eagle . . . but a scrappy sparrow? They're a dime a dozen. Jesus said so Himself.
>
> Yet from thousands of bird species, the Lord chose the most insignificant, least-noticed, scruffiest bird of all. A pint-sized thing that even dedicated birdwatchers ignore.
>
> That thought alone calmed my fears. I felt significant

> and noticed. . . . If the great God of heaven concerns Himself with a ragtag little sparrow clinging to the bird feeder outside my window, He cares about you.[13]

In the world's eyes, a sparrow may be worth just half a Roman penny, but our Savior who holds all things together—never failing to notice the finest details of the smallest bird—will never fail to care for you. So be anxious for nothing. You, my friend, are worth more than many sparrows.

— CHAPTER 14 —

Mockingbird Maturity

Whatever you have learned or received or heard from me, or seen in me—put it into practice. And the God of peace will be with you.

—PHILIPPIANS 4:9

It is not great talents God blesses so much as great likeness to Jesus.

—ROBERT MURRAY M'CHEYNE[1]

IT'S EARLY MORNING at my campsite in the Smokies; I'm barely awake and too cold to willingly surrender the warmth of my sleeping bag just yet. Of course that doesn't mean I can't get an early jump on my day with a little birding by ear. From inside my tent I listen to the flute-like melody of the Hermit Thrush that just woke me up. He's quickly followed by the *bird-ee bird-ee bird-ee* of a Northern Cardinal, and the *pita-pita* of a Tufted Titmouse. Oddly though, they all sound like they're coming from the same branch. Realization dawns: This chorus of birds perched above my tent is actually *one* bird. One unbelievably proficient bird.

The Northern Mockingbird is a bird stuffed full of songs, and its scientific name is well-chosen: *Mimus polyglottos,* Latin for "many-tongued mimic." The mockingbird only has one tongue, thankfully, but it has seven pairs of syrinx muscles, resulting in impressive voice control. This gray-and-white virtuoso can reproduce the sounds of over a hundred and fifty birds. And why stop there? Mockingbirds can also reproduce the sounds of chirping crickets, peeping frogs, meowing cats, and barking dogs. Observers have noted instances of mockingbirds imitating ringing phones, car alarms, and squeaky pulley wheels. A mockingbird was spotted at an outdoor concert-in-the-park symphony trying to imitate the violin. One homeowner watched a mockingbird simulate the predatory sound of a Northern Harrier, scaring all the other birds out of the yard so it could enjoy the spoils of the vacant feeder. Another shared about a mockingbird that imitated the sound of her gate opening one morning, prompting her laughter, then the bird's imitation of her laughter, then her laughter at the impression of her laughter.

Thomas Jefferson had a pet mockingbird named Dick, one of America's more unusual White House residents. Dick could sing popular tunes to Jefferson while he napped and, while accompanying him on a trip to Paris, learned to imitate the creaking of the ship's timbers. Today, the mockingbird maintains its political interests by serving as the state bird of Arkansas, Florida, Mississippi, Tennessee, and Texas—as well as a brief stint as the state bird of South Carolina from 1939 to 1948 before getting voted out of office by the Carolina Wren. (I don't know about you, but the thought of elected officials having a wren versus mockingbird debate on the state senate floor sounds like a refreshingly simpler political climate.)

With all that imitation, it's helpful to know that the mockingbird does have, in poker terms, a tell. All three mimics from the Eastern United States do. The Gray Catbird's repertoire consists of quick unrepeated phrases interspersed with a spastic "meow." The Brown Thrasher sings its borrowed songs in pairs, each tune sung only and exactly twice before moving on to the next one. The mockingbird can't stop at two but is usually done by four or five. If you hear three rounds of a cardinal that suddenly starts speaking chickadee, it's safe to assume you've been hoodwinked by a mockingbird. But even if you're wise to the pattern, it's still easy to get scammed—even the Merlin app from the Cornell Lab of Ornithology regularly misidentifies mockingbird song.

Maybe imitation is flattery, but the mockingbird isn't trying to flatter us—or to mock us, for that matter. In Harper Lee's book-defining quote, Miss Maudie explains to Scout that "it's a sin to kill a mockingbird" because they "don't do one thing but make music for us to enjoy. They don't eat up people's gardens, don't nest in corncribs, they don't do one thing but sing their hearts out for us."[2] Their song is a gift and we're the recipients.

But the mockingbird offers more than just a heartfelt repertoire. If you're like me, you desire to keep learning and growing. The mockingbird sings to show you how it's done; listen in and you'll hear the secrets of a lifelong learner.

Mimicry as Maturity

The mockingbird is always listening for tunes to commit to memory. While the majority of birds seem content to carefully recite the same song imprinted as a chick, or even learned while still in the egg, the mockingbird has a growth mindset. It never stops adding tunes to its set list. Maybe you can't teach an old dog new tricks, but the mockingbird is always up for a new song. That's why this bird is such a fitting embodiment of Paul's words in Philippians 4:

> Finally, brothers and sisters, whatever is true, whatever is noble, whatever is right, whatever is pure, whatever is lovely, whatever is admirable—if anything is excellent or praiseworthy—think about such things. Whatever you have learned or received or heard from me, or seen in me—put it into practice. And the God of peace will be with you. (Philippians 4:8–9)

Paul wants his readers to seek out the best things to imitate. Listen for the admirable and praiseworthy. Learn to speak the language of what's pure, right, and lovely. Commit to memory the words that are true and noble, working them into your thoughts, words, and actions. If you're marked by this pursuit, the mockingbird is an apt metaphor for you—a perpetual learner and a mascot of good-to-great growth.

I remember, as a young seminary student, listening in as two fellow seminarians discussed the importance of imitating mentors. I was incensed. "Why would I want anyone to imitate *me*? We want people to imitate Jesus, not each other."

One of these friends patiently pointed me to Philippians 4:9: "Whatever you have learned or received or heard from me, or seen in me—put it into practice." Paul says the same thing in the previous chapter: "Join together in following my example, brothers and sisters, and just as you have us as a model, keep your eyes on those who live as we do" (Philippians 3:17). And the letter to the Philippians is not an isolated case. Paul challenges his readers to follow his lead in 1 Corinthians 4:16 ("Therefore I urge you to imitate me") and 11:1 ("Follow my example, as I follow the example of Christ") and elsewhere. Discipleship is a picture of imitation. The Greek word for "imitate" comes from the same root as the mockingbird's Latin name: *Mimos.* Mimic. Discipleship is mimicry.

The needed disclaimer in those verses, of course, is "as I follow Christ." Imitation is a given, but what will we pass on? What will we pick up? The handoff doesn't always go as expected. Generally speaking, the act of imitation can go awry when either (1) the student fails to follow the teacher's example or (2) the teacher fails to set an example worth following.

In the first case, imitation becomes distortion. Positive things, when copied improperly, produce negative results. When a pastor pawns off another pastor's sermon as his own, it's called plagiarism. When a moviegoer secretly films the theater screen with his iPhone, it's called piracy. When an underground printing press cranks out twenty-dollar bills, it's called counterfeiting. When a friend passes on a juicy tidbit they heard about so-and-so, it's called gossip. These dark forms of imitation *take* something. They take credit; they take intellectual property; they take someone's reputation. But imitation—in its best forms—*gives.*

In the second case, imitation breaks down because the teacher sets a poor example. Have you noticed how much easier it is to pass along our vices than our virtues? Parents are especially conscious of this as they strive to set worthy examples for their children. Of all the things my kids hear from me, will they remember my patient, compassionate, "Dad of the

Year" conversations or my habit of yelling at NFL referees through the TV screen? My believable words are those reinforced by my actions; time will tell which ones they truly are.

I'm reminded of one of the great mimics of Australia, the cockatoo. Reports began surfacing in the outback of wild cockatoos calling out curse words. The phenomenon apparently began when a domesticated cockatoo escaped. It had a few choice words it had learned in captivity that it apparently passed along to its new flock. I'm sure the bird heard plenty of human words during its time with people, but the ones it remembered reveal a lot about its former owner.[3]

It Bears Repeating

The fact that imitation can go wrong was a major motivation for Paul to live out a Christ-honoring walk. He wrote elsewhere that he and his colleagues lived faithfully "in order to offer ourselves as a model for you to imitate" (2 Thessalonians 3:9). He was regularly concerned with modeling the example of Jesus, aware that his not-yet-glorified nature still bore its share of inconsistencies. But he asked those around him to watch for the aspects of his life that showcased the character and nature of his Lord. What might those be? Philippians 4 gives us a great list: whatever is true, noble, right, pure, lovely, admirable, excellent, and praiseworthy. And ultimately, aren't those eight adjectives simply descriptions of our Savior? In the end, Paul's list is really a call to pursue the character of Christ—the One who is all these things and more.

That character is lived out in part, albeit imperfectly, in the lives of the people around us. Paul points to Jesus *through* the exemplified life of others, asking his readers to recognize the "praiseworthy" in Epaphroditus (Philippians 2:30) or the "admirable" in Timothy (Philippians 2:22). He's still pointing his flashlight in the same direction—toward Christ—but the beam is passing through the lens of another person's life. "Imitate *us* on this one, folks, because we're trying to show you what imitating Jesus looks like."

So ask yourself: How am *I* growing in Christlikeness by imitating others? And how are others growing in Christlikeness by imitating *me*?

As a follower of Jesus, you need someone to copy. There's nothing surprising about this fact because it's true in every aspect of life. If you want to become a better golfer, you hire a coach. If you want to learn guitar, you find a good instructor. If you want to learn a language, you find a fluent speaker. Even masters of their craft have coaches and mentors (paradoxically, experts typically seek *more* training, not less). Here's the point: If you want to grow spiritually in a particular area, it requires learning from someone more mature. If you want a better marriage, identify a couple whose marriage you respect and ask to spend time with them to better understand what makes their relationship tick. If you desire more patience, identify a noticeably patient person in your life and start asking questions. If you struggle to understand how to faithfully shepherd your kids, ask other parents about their family rhythms of discipleship. Why are we so reticent to ask? Is it embarrassment? Pride? If we learn golf from golfers and music from musicians, shouldn't we learn faith from the faithful?

On the flip side, what might others learn from *you*? Where is God growing you for the sake of others? How can you pass along the mockingbird tunes you've learned to sing? A critic of Tim Keller's preaching once said to him, "When you are well prepared for your sermon, you cite a great variety of sources, but when you aren't well prepared, you just quote C. S. Lewis."[4] While that could be seen as incriminating—and a convicting word on adequate sermon preparation—to me it's actually inspiring. The authors and influences we know best flow from us naturally. They reveal the deep and familiar well we most readily draw from. Keller knew Lewis so well that, when other voices weren't as obvious, Lewis just spilled out of him.

So what spills out of *me*? This is convicting. Do I know more movie lines than I know lines of Scripture? Are my factory settings set to the language of my Savior? Has my mind dwelt on what is pure, noble, excellent, and praiseworthy so much that it becomes repeatable at the default level? Am I learning songs worthy of repetition?

Repeat the Sounding Joy

The eminent theologian (and lifelong birder) John Stott was once asked by a reporter, "You've had a brilliant academic career; first at Cambridge, Rector at twenty-nine, Chaplain to the Queen; what is your ambition now?"

Stott simply replied, "To be more like Jesus."

Tim Chester summarizes, "This is what Stott found compelling about Christianity. As we see Christ's glory, we want to serve him; as we see his beauty, we want to imitate him."[5] A Christian's greatest aspiration is mimicry—pursuing a deeper and deeper Christlikeness, motivated by his worthiness, until the day we fully reflect him.

In a sense, Jesus's message was mimicry too. He told the disciples, "I no longer call you servants, because a servant does not know his master's business. Instead, I have called you friends, for everything that I learned from my Father I have made known to you" (John 15:15). He listened to the Father's song and repeated it note for note to his disciples. Don't ever assume the will of the Father and Son are at odds even for a moment. Impossible. Jesus's actions, teachings, and character repeat the sounding joy of the Great I Am. Even the Cross of Christ sings the song of our Father's loving heart. Especially so, in fact.

And he sends his Spirit to do the same: "When he, the Spirit of truth, comes, he will guide you into all the truth. He will not speak on his own; he will speak only what he hears, and he will tell you what is yet to come" (John 16:13). God the Son and God the Spirit perfectly repeat the heart of the Father into our lives. They sing a united song in perfect resonance with one another. Every stanza of that song—every true, noble, right, pure, lovely, admirable, excellent, and praiseworthy note—is worthy of emulation.

— CHAPTER 15 —

The Strength of Eagles

I have learned the secret of being content in any and every situation, whether well fed or hungry, whether living in plenty or in want. I can do all this through him who gives me strength.

—PHILIPPIANS 4:12–13

"Farewell!" they cried, "Wherever you fare, till your eyries receive you at the journey's end!" That is the polite thing to say among eagles.

—J.R.R. TOLKIEN[1]

AND NOW WE come to the most familiar verse in the book of Philippians and one of the top-ten most quoted verses in the whole Bible: "I can do all things through him who strengthens me."[2] You'll find this verse cross-stitched in kitchens, decorating office cubicles, or adorning team locker rooms. It's the verse Christians quote before marathons, bungee jumps, or long airline flights next to a crying toddler. We recite it in the places we need strength.

And so, as we contemplate the power God gives, I'd like to recommend two candidates for the bird mascot for strength. One will be obvious and the other one not so much. Both are accurate pictures of power but in very different ways, and one might bring us closer to understanding the sort of power Paul describes in these verses so we can better experience it as well.

The Wings of Power

Is there a better image of power and strength among birds than the eagle? Today, across six continents, eagles evoke the image of aerial domination. The Harpy Eagle of Central and South America has been called "a Sherman tank with fighter-jet wings"[3] and can lift up to forty pounds. The Wedge-tailed Eagle of Australia has a wingspan of over nine feet and can take down a kangaroo. And the Cornell Lab of Ornithology aptly describes Europe's enormous White-tailed Eagle with this highly scientific observation: "Looks like a flying barn door."[4] Just one talon on a Bald Eagle can exert a pressure of four hundred pounds per square inch, enough to snap a human femur. The first-century naturalist Pliny the Elder suggested that if you put an eagle feather in a box with other assorted bird feathers, the eagle's would "devour and consume all the rest."[5] Funny guy, that Pliny.

The phrase *eagle eye* reminds us that this bird's strength goes well beyond its wings and talons to its powerful vision. The apostle John was depicted as an eagle in religious art and illuminated manuscripts (such as the Lindisfarne Gospels and the Book of Kells) because of the way his writings peer into the future. It's believed that eagles can spot moving prey up to three miles away and track a rodent by the ultraviolet rays reflected in its urine. Once when visiting a raptor center, I was told that their resident Bald Eagles could read the inscription on a quarter from fifty yards away. (I was impressed by their eyesight but even more so by the fact that someone had taught them how to read.)

The eagle is undeniably a power bird.[6] That makes them a go-to symbol for companies seeking to inject some strength and confidence into their logos. Insurance companies. Airlines. Breweries. The Ramones. The Roman Empire. The eagle is the national bird of seventeen countries and the most popular mascot in U.S. college sports. The United States has claimed the Bald Eagle as its national emblem since 1782 (although surprisingly it wasn't officially named our national bird until being signed into law on Christmas Eve 2024). Over the years, the U.S. government has co-opted the eagle into pretty much every logo we can think of, including for the Air Force, Marines, Central Intelligence Agency, Postal Service, Department of Justice, and Internal Revenue Service. Yes, even taxes are better with eagles.

When we turn our attention to the Scriptures, we see a similar show of power when the eagle appears. Other than the dove (whose references are usually post-mortem), no bird is referenced more often in the Bible than the eagle, and the image is usually one of no-nonsense muscle. Every major prophet invokes the eagle, along with three of the minor ones.

Eagles foretell the swiftness of opposing armies (Jeremiah 4:13), the menace of judgment (Hosea 8:1), or the impenetrability of fortresses (Jeremiah 49:16; Obadiah 4). In the book of Job, eagles are soaring emblems of God's perplexing control (Job 39:27–30), and in Proverbs they're one of Agur's top-four jaw-dropping mysteries of life (Proverbs 30:18–19).

The eagle's strength is ominous, mysterious. Scripturally, when an eagle spreads its wings, it's generally a good time to reconsider your life choices and make amends. Of course, it's a different thing entirely if that strength is working *for* you, not *against* you. Consider, for instance, the well-known words of Isaiah 40:31:

> Those who hope in the LORD
>   will renew their strength.
> They will soar on wings like eagles;
>   they will run and not grow weary,
>   they will walk and not be faint.

That wouldn't be a bad verse to put next to Philippians 4:13 in the team locker room, would it? It's a divine promise of endurance—a God who gives us the strength we need to thrive. The image is equally reassuring in Deuteronomy 32:10–11, as God describes the exodus in eagle terms:

> He shielded him and cared for him;
>   he guarded him as the apple of his eye,
> like an eagle that stirs up its nest
>   and hovers over its young,
> that spreads its wings to catch them
>   and carries them aloft.

When God says he "carries them aloft" like an eagle, he's using a metaphor of mightiness—a God who's willing to carry a whole nation on his back. That has the same tenderhearted feel as Isaiah's imagery, right? Yes... unless you're Egypt. God reminded Israel, "You yourselves have seen what I did to Egypt, and how I carried you on eagles' wings and brought you to myself" (Exodus 19:4). Those wings famously left behind ten plagues' worth of carnage as they lifted a nation of slaves to freedom. Good for them, bad for Egypt. Like I said, an eagle's strength can work *for* you or *against* you. Either way, it's a rugged image of muscular power.

But is this the sort of strength Paul's talking about in Philippians 4:13?

Extraordinary Strength for Ordinary Stuff

"I can do all things through him who strengthens me" sounds like a mighty-eagle sort of verse. Read it at the gym and you'll be tempted to flex. Read it in the halftime locker room, with a rousing sing-along of "I Believe I Can Fly," and maybe your team will turn the game around. And don't get me wrong; all things truly *are* possible when you have a miracle-working Savior.

It's not *less* than that, but it's also *more* than that. Philippians 4:13 is not an invincibility suit or a guarantee of crossing the finish line first.

It's better.

The problem is that our vision for this verse is often far too nearsighted. We ask God to strengthen our capacities or willpower for a given situation, task, event, medical setback, you name it. God loves to show up in those places with his mighty eagle wings. But those scenarios are victory for a *moment,* while Paul has an ongoing empowerment in mind—a power that will not only sustain us *during* challenges but will equip the way we *perceive* them.

What is this ongoing power? Look at the context. Before he says he can do all things through Christ, Paul writes, "I have learned to be content whatever the circumstances. I know what it is to be in need, and I know what it is to have plenty. I have learned the secret of being content in any and every situation, whether well fed or hungry, whether living in plenty or in want" (Philippians 4:11–12). Do you see how much grander that verse is when set against the life lesson Paul's giving us? It's not about the arduous tasks of running half-marathons or getting through Friday traffic; it's about the much more arduous task of finding *contentment* in every circumstance.

Does that sound somehow *lesser* to us? The strength to *do* feels mighty, with talons and fireworks and swelling guitar solos. The strength to *be* feels mundane, disappointing, the sound of air being let out of a balloon. Contentment feels too ordinary. Yes, the Bible is full of promises to fuel our *doing*. But this is not one of them.

Contentment is a rare kind of strength. If you're honest, which is harder for you: obtaining a momentary victory or living a lifestyle of contentment? Which one do you need more? Before you answer that, let me offer a definition. The Puritan Jeremiah Burroughs defined contentment as "that sweet, inward, quiet, gracious frame of spirit, which freely submits to and delights in God's wise and fatherly disposal in every condition."[7] I stumbled on Burroughs's book *The Rare Jewel of Christian Contentment* at a key season of my own discontent, still single in my mid-thirties. I struggled to trust God's goodness because, to be honest, I could imagine a *better* goodness. In that season, my friends would've told you I had elevated bachelor-whining to an art form. But Burroughs's encouragements were a regular refrain to grow my confidence in God's sovereign goodness in the harder moments of my discontent. It was a call for me to regularly ask myself, "Do I really trust what a sovereign and loving God is doing in me? Can I submit to and delight in God's wise and fatherly disposal?" I discovered those to be far better questions than my various forms of "Why me?" In asking trust-themed questions, I wasn't just seeking changed circumstances but a changed heart.

I'm convinced that contentment fundamentally comes down to this question: Do we believe God truly has our best in mind? If so, we can receive whatever he chooses to give. We can trust and let the canvas of our hearts submit to God's frame. Easier said than done, I know; after all, "God's wise and fatherly disposal" is a perspective we lack, and sometimes our scenarios don't seem to measure up to the "life to the full" Jesus talks about (see John 10:10), at least not as *we* would define it if we were him. Trust usually means we don't have all the answers. There are holes in the plot that we must commit to the Lord to fill in.

But the unfathomable reality that Jesus is *for* us has already been well-attested—on a cross. Author Paige Benton Brown asks, "Can God be any less good to me on the average Tuesday morning than he was on that monumental Friday afternoon when he hung on a cross in my place?" By no means! "God will not be less good to me . . . because God *cannot* be less good to me. . . . It is a cosmic impossibility for God to shortchange any of his children."[8] If God has already given us his Son (Romans 8:32), along with forgiveness, adoption, and the promise of resurrection, how much more committed to our good could he possibly be? Our faith in those realities will settle our discontented heart.

This is what Paul means when he says "I can do all things through him who strengthens me." It's the strength to rest contentedly in God "whatever the circumstances." Yes, I can win through him who strengthens me. But I can also *lose* through him who strengthens me. I can be healed of my disease or endure it. I can take the gain or bear the loss. I can nail the job interview or deal with the disappointment by trusting the Lord to provide a different way. I can feel his strength equally in first place or last place, on eagle's wings or dodo's wings.

It doesn't mean I have to love my scenario; Burroughs also recorded the paradoxical sentence "I am content with what I have, and hope for better."[9] In Christ we can contentedly be single and still waiting, unemployed and still looking, bedridden and still seeking healing. In fact, there's a sense in which Christians should be the most discontented people on the planet. After all, we long for the day when faith is made sight, justice reigns, and truth wins. In the words of U2, we "believe in the kingdom come" but "still haven't found what [we're] looking for."[10] We know the day will come. In the meantime, we can endure the *now* through him who gives us strength.

A Different Kind of Strength

Let's return briefly to the question of potential candidates for the bird mascot of strength. If this verse were about the power to achieve, endure, and win the day, the eagle would do nicely. But if—as I've suggested—verse 13 is talking about the strength of a contented heart, then I believe we need a different picture. It has to be a strength that's less like a superhero movie and more like a day in the life. Less like a bird of prey and more like (bear with me on this one) a Mallard.

The Mallard is a type of duck known as a "dabbling duck." While some ducks are built for diving deep, with feet positioned toward the rear for stronger propulsion, dabblers have legs located closer to the center of their bodies, allowing them to walk more naturally and even feed terrestrially. You won't see a merganser or a scoter strolling onto shore to mooch your breadcrumbs; they're simply not built well for land. But a Mallard can make the transition from water to land easily. Granted, it's more of a waddle, which might not be the most elegant strut in the animal kingdom, but it gets the job done.

Of course, they're also adept swimmers, even without that deep-dive capacity. Since they're happy feeding on the surface, tipping forward to nibble shallow aquatic plants or insect larvae, there's really no need for them to plunge the depths, and a Mallard is probably happiest when bobbing on the surface of a pond or marsh.

When it's time to leave, Mallards can effortlessly lift off and take to the sky. Migrating flocks clock in at up to fifty-five miles per hour, their rear-built wings carrying them for hours at a time. The average Mallard migrates nine hundred miles in a season; one transmitter-fitted bird even went that far in a single day.[11]

The Mallard doesn't do any of this in world-record fashion. It doesn't swim the deepest or run the fastest or fly the farthest. Instead it "dabbles" in all three. What other birds can do that? It's a short list. Think about it. Eagles are powerful in the sky but flail to get airborne if they get below the water's surface on a fishing attempt. A songbird owns the skies but drowns if you fill the birdbath up too much. A loon owns the water but is helpless on land, while a penguin owns the ice but can't fly. The Chimney Swift, a mesmerizing king of the air, can barely perch on land, let alone walk. Most birds navigate one element or maybe two. But the Mallard is equally comfortable in all three.

In elementary school I had a pet Mallard, a rescue from a nearby lake (let's call him Quacker, since that was his name). We dug a small pond in the backyard—more of a gross muddy puddle, really—and despite his sloppy living conditions, Quacker seemed content to call it home. He stood dutifully beside me at the mailbox each morning while I waited for the school bus, to the sneers (and secret jealousies, I'd bet) of the onlooking passengers. After the bus picked me up, he'd happily waddle back to his godforsaken puddle.

My point is this. In Christ, we can be equally at home and at peace regardless of the environment we find ourselves in. He will equip our discontented heart with a settled strength that breathes deep of his grace—in sickness or in health, in plenty or in want, for richer or for poorer, roadside or puddle-side. The strength Jesus gave Paul was the capacity to look with contentment on all he was and all he had because of all he was and all he had in Jesus.

That's the strength Jesus offers you as well.

Business author Ken Blanchard has popularly said, "Don't quack like a duck. Soar like an eagle."[12] Don't you believe it. While the eagle rightly evokes our admiration and awe, we'd do well to emulate the contented strength of the duck.

— CHAPTER 16 —

The Provision of Ravens

My God will meet all your needs according to the riches of his glory in Christ Jesus.

—PHILIPPIANS 4:19

And though the darkness and the dearth
May threaten life and light,
Remember God still rules the earth,
And ravens fly at night.

—JOHN PIPER[1]

JUST AS WE'VE gotten comfortable with the idea of Jesus asking us to "look at the birds of the air" (Matthew 6:26), the gospel of Luke gives the command a jarring spin. The lesson is essentially the same, but the subject matter somehow feels less like hope and more like Halloween: "Consider the *ravens*" (Luke 12:24).

That changes things, doesn't it? Author Debbie Blue writes, "Matthew's 'birds of the air' might seem light and sweet somehow; look at all the colorful things flittering and chirping and singing, all little and cute. Considering the raven is a different affair.... People describing the raven's voice often say, 'It sounds like death.'"[2] The raven is not an obvious mascot for a worry-free life. Instead it's a feature character in Gothic horror, violent Norse mythology, and modern dystopian fiction. When the bird shows up in *The Hobbit, Maleficent, Snow White,* or *Game of Thrones,* go ahead and cue the ominous music. When it appears in Shakespeare's *Julius Caesar, Othello, Hamlet,* or *Macbeth,* it's a literary harbinger of death. In Proverbs 30:17 it's a grotesque agent of judgment for breaking the fifth commandment. Its widespread appearances in folklore depict it as the ghost of a murder victim (Sweden), a tragically damned soul (Germany), or a dangerous shape-shifting hag (Scotland). In the Quran, a raven teaches Cain how to bury Abel's body—a pretty creepy skill to put on your résumé. And don't forget Edgar Allan Poe, who painted the bird as the mocking personification of unrelenting grief. By most accounts, the raven is a menacing trickster. A flock is called either an *unkindness* or a *conspiracy*—kind of foreboding either way you go.

But hey, by all means, consider the ravens.

What would Jesus have us learn from this "grim, ungainly, ghastly, gaunt, and ominous bird of yore"?[3] Like Matthew's sparrow, it seems Jesus wants us to understand the provision of God (see chapter 13). He reminds us that ravens "do not sow or reap, they have no storeroom or barn; yet God feeds them"—a reality that informs our faith so we don't worry. When we tally up the Bible's raven references, we discover that this bird is perfectly suited to deliver this lesson.

Raven Rations

Three times in Scripture we're told that God provides food for the ravens. Aside from the Luke reference, the theme also appears in God's monologue to Job in Job 38:41:

> Who provides food for the raven
>   when its young cry out to God
>   and wander about for lack of food?

God reminds Job of his absolute power. Granted, Job might have preferred a straight answer on the problem of evil. Instead, God waxes eloquent on the ibis, rooster, ostrich, raven, stork, hawk, and eagle; "You want answers, Job? I give you *birds*!" It's a passage that makes an ornitheologist quite happy. Throughout the whole monologue, the question is provision and the answer is God. Job seeks the *why* and God gives the *who*. That's a common script for God, both in the Bible and in our personal experiences. God answers the *why* with the *who* because the most important thing we need when we're suffering isn't more understanding but more of *him*. And that's enough for Job to trust again.

The same image appears in Psalm 147:9:

> He provides food for the cattle
>   and for the young ravens when they call.

The point of these verses is far richer than "God loves baby ravens." His compassion toward his creatures reminds us that a good Father knows how to give good gifts. If he's attentive to the little beaks in a raven's nest, how much more is he committed to his people?

But there's a fourth provision-of-ravens verse as well, and in this one God turns the tables. Yes, God provides *for* ravens, but sometimes he also provides *through* them. In 1 Kings 17 we're introduced to the prophet Elijah, a man on the run from Ahab, the most heinous Israelite king in the history of heinous Israelite kings. Before heading into witness protection in the region of Gilead across the Jordan, Elijah's parting words to the king warn that it will only rain in Israel if God tells Elijah to speak it into being. This authority is a slap in the face to the god of the age, Ba'al, whose followers believed controlled the crop cycle. Elijah predicts a three-year drought, which would render Ba'al impotent, remind the people who is truly in charge, and perhaps give the king second thoughts about his blatant idolatry.[4] It's a hard providence, but when repentance is the goal, drought can be grace.

Elijah, by contrast, will not go thirsty. God sends his prophet into the wilderness of Gilead and promises, "You will drink from the brook, and I have directed the ravens to supply you with food there" (1 Kings 17:4). In Poe's famous poem, the raven was asked, "Is there balm in Gilead?"

"Quoth the Raven, 'Nevermore.'"

But for Elijah, is there balm in Gilead? Quoth the raven, "Yup, got ya covered."

There's something appropriate yet unnerving about Elijah's DoorDash service. On the plus side, scientists agree that ravens might be the most intelligent bird on the planet, capable of some impressively complex tasks. Ravens don't just make tools; they make tools that they use to make other tools. They plan ahead. They have astounding social memory, remembering old bird friends up to three years after parting ways.[5] They even possess the capacity to console one another, demonstrating sympathetic concern for injured members of the flock.[6] And their spatial memory is unbelievably advanced, remembering exactly where they stored away treasured items.

On the con side, well, they're ravens—grim and ominous, "the bird of doom and deluge."[7] More than that, they're a strange choice for a law-abiding Israelite prophet because for the Jews, ravens were *unclean.* Moses specifically cites them in the life list of taboo birds presented in Leviticus 11 and Deuteronomy 14. Thou shalt not eat a raven. Presumably that's because a raven eats dead things, and scavengers are ceremonially unclean: dirty birds. We'd rightly expect that label to include the daily bread-and-meat rations they're delivering in those unclean beaks. Some Bible commentaries on this passage explain that the provision of meat for Elijah was a luxurious delicacy. I sort of doubt it. True, ravens are opportunistic feeders that will eat plenty of things, including live prey, but they're especially known as carrion eaters, as any number of pirate- or Western-movie gallows scenes will attest. With God all things are possible, and so it's possible Elijah was eating medium-rare filet mignon, but it's equally possible he learned to cook it extra-well-done and never ask where it came from. Either way, God provides a banquet in the wilderness.

Consider the ravens. They're such an unlikely picture of God's provision, yet the Bible shows us that God provides *for* them and *through* them. He doesn't always provide the way we might expect. He uses "the lowly things of this world and the despised things" to surprise us "so that no one may boast before him" (1 Corinthians 1:28–29). In this unusual Bible story, we can see ourselves as Elijah, receiving answers to prayer from unexpected sources. But we can just as easily see ourselves as the raven: the undeservingly despised whom God gives the dignity of purpose and service as we humbly meet the needs of others.

What We Really Need

At the close of Paul's letter to the Philippians, he confidently proclaims God's provision in his own life and in theirs: "My God will meet all your needs according to the riches of his glory in Christ Jesus" (Philippians 4:19). Sadly, if verse 13 ("I can do all things through him who gives me strength") is the most misused verse in the Bible, verse 19 might be a close second. The church of cha-ching is quick to interpret "all your needs" as a blank check, a name-it-and-claim-it verse that proves that God wants to make you crazy wealthy, as long as you have enough faith or follow the right formula.

But the context of these verses doesn't let us get away with that. Rather than seeking our own prosperity, this passage is all about audaciously others-centered generosity. The Philippians financially support Paul out of their *poverty,* so much so that elsewhere Paul describes them by saying, "In the midst of a very severe trial, their overflowing joy and their extreme poverty welled up in rich generosity. For I testify that they gave as much as they were able, and even beyond their ability. Entirely on their own, they urgently pleaded with us for the privilege of sharing in this service to the Lord's people" (2 Corinthians 8:2–4). The Philippians aren't living large by modern Western wealth standards—or even first-century standards.

And neither is Paul. He precedes this comment about God meeting *their* needs by asserting that God has already met *his.* He claims to "have received full payment and have more than enough. I am amply supplied" (Philippians 4:18). Paul's got surplus, some cushy financial margin. It sounds comfortably middle-class until we remember that he's writing from *prison*. Although he's living a scenario that most of us would consider destitute, he says with no irony that his every need is supplied. Even in a drought, the ravens keep flying in with daily bread.

Will God meet all your needs? Absolutely yes . . . and also no. Yes, he will, but he'll do so by *his* definition, not ours. Like Job, sometimes we don't know what we need, expecting a quick escape from hardship when what we truly need is deeper trust, patience, or humility. For instance, when the Lord moved my wife and me from our church in Orlando to a new ministry in Charlotte, I remember how confidently we believed all the pieces would fall quickly and neatly into place. This move was, after all, God's very evident call, confirmed in dozens of ways. But when our house in Florida didn't sell nearly as quickly as I thought, I began to doubt. "Lord, we *need* you to sell our house so others will see how you're paving the way for this move and give you the glory for it." The almost-audible response was "Well, I also get the glory when two people learn how to trust me more deeply without quick answers." What we thought we needed wasn't what we *really* needed.

God is far more concerned with forming the character of Christ in us than he is with the power bill, although he's committed to meet those physical needs too (and yes, our house eventually sold). As I said in the last chapter, Paul's confidence that God will provide is ultimately about contentment, which is a reminder to us that our greatest possession isn't our cash on hand but our satisfaction in the glory of God. For Paul, it wasn't *really* about the gift. By the standards of the typical thank-you note, his words here might even feel borderline rude: "Not that I desire your gifts; what I desire is that more be credited to your account" (Philippians 4:17).

Imagine getting a thank-you note in the mail from some newlyweds that says, "Dear friends, thank you for the soup tureen. To be honest, we didn't need it. Actually, we were pretty content without it. But we're glad you're learning how to be generous because that's good for you, so we're going to keep it." In essence, that's what Paul does. To a church that has just given extravagantly out of their poverty, he writes in Philippians 4:11 that he didn't need the gift and in verse 17 that he wasn't seeking it. But what the gift reveals about their spiritual growth is the *real* provision. God is growing the Philippians in rich generosity and faithful trust, "and because of this I rejoice" (Philippians 1:18). Both Paul and the Philippians remain detached from the money they have: Paul refuses to base his contentment on it, and the Philippians refuse to keep it to themselves.

If you think of yourself as the raven in these various references, you're more likely to see yourself on the receiving end of God's provision—the young bird with the open beak. That's fine, God's promises are ironclad, and Jesus meant to encourage us with that image. But where is the Lord calling you to be on the delivery end, a raven who brings God's provision into the wilderness to meet the needs of others? There are Elijahs out there who need meat and bread. Every day is an opportunity to be the hands and feet (and raven wings) of Jesus.

Good News for the Ravenous

Ravens don't just deliver provision though. They deliver *news*. Stephen Moss writes, "Ravens also have a long and distinguished history as portentous messengers."[8] Greek mythology contains stories of Apollo using these birds to carry messages. In Norse mythology the direction is reversed, with Odin on the receiving end. His two ravens, Huginn and Muninn ("Thought" and "Memory"), travel the world to spy it out and return to perch on his shoulders and whisper breaking news into his ears. In more recent myth, the ravens at the Tower of London are alleged to control the fate of the British Empire. If they ever leave the Tower, it's said that the monarchy will fall. No wonder their wings are clipped.[9] The remaining biblical reference to ravens is featured in the Noah's ark narrative, where the raven is the first bird released to find dry ground. While the dove (who gets her chance when the raven fails to return) tends to be presented as the helpful hero, we should probably admit that the raven accomplished its messenger duties, at least sort of; if it hadn't found land, it would have had to return to the ark, so its disappearance informed Noah that the waters were receding. A postcard would have been nice though.

Those raven roles are all about carrying *news,* be it the hope of a receding flood or the hint of a collapsing empire. And the core of the Christian faith is the proclamation of news: "good news of great joy" (Luke 2:10, ESV). The Christian message is often demoted to the realm of mere advice about the good life. But the word *gospel* means "good news." As I said in the prologue, that's different from every other philosophical or religious system. Good advice might contain wisdom, but it leaves the outcomes up to us. Good *news,* on the other hand, isn't something we do; it's something we believe and receive. What we could not do, impeded by our sin nature and in fact dead in it (Romans 8:3; Ephesians 2:1), Jesus did on our behalf—a perfectly obedient life credited to us by faith with the jaw-dropping promises of no condemnation and life to the full (Romans 8:1; John 10:10). It's not about what we do to get to God but what he's done to get to us.

If you consistently leave your Sunday morning sermon having been told what to do without also being told what Christ has already done, you may need to prayerfully consider whether your church has become a place of "neither dew nor rain" (1 Kings 17:1). Pastor Tim Keller taught that although he had preached thousands of sermons, all of them essentially consisted of the same basic "metaoutline"—a "deep gospel pattern" that says (1) this is what we need to do, (2) this is why we can't do it, (3) this is how Jesus did it, and (4) this is how we live in it, through him.[10] Many sermons stop after the first point. But that's not good news.

By definition, the appetites of ravens are ravenous. Our penchant for sin, likewise, is a ravenous appetite. Our wants are misplaced, and our hearts are prone to wander, hungering after lesser affections. Admitting this reality isn't about low self-esteem but freedom; it makes the good news even better. Jesus died for our ravenous idolatries. Debbie Blue writes, "God feeds the ravens, the ravenous, the mixed-up greedy glutton carrion eater. That's saying a lot more, somehow—something more shocking, maybe, than that God's willing to give bird food to light eaters. And how much more will God feed us?"[11] Our raven-feeding God provides for the unlikely and undeserving, giving not just daily bread but the bread of eternal life, a life united to a resurrected Savior. "Sin had left a crimson stain; He washed it white as snow."[12]

Banquet in the Wilderness

When you consider God's amazing provision for you, don't forget that if he never gave you another gift, another grace, another answered prayer, he has already given you enough by giving you the gift of the righteousness of his Son. By faith he treats you as if his Son's righteousness was your own track record. He treats your debt of sin as fully reconciled on a Roman cross. You are granted access to the throne room, a claim to the family name, and a place setting at the final feast. These things have been given to you by your faith in Jesus.

But there's more good news... He is *still* actively giving. He's not done yet. "He who did not spare his own Son, but gave him up for us all—how will he not also, along with him, graciously give us all things?" (Romans 8:32). There are more ravens on the way, bearing gifts and grace and good news and new mercies every morning.

John Piper poeticized the Elijah story this way:

> But then God said, "You will not die.
> Consider how the ravens fly:
> Are they not free at my command
> To go and come from Ahab's land,
> And carry here bread, meat and all
> Through windows in the castle wall?
> And will I not then care for you?
> Consider now what I can do:
> Henceforth I make of your distress
> A banquet in the wilderness." . . .
>
> And though the darkness and the dearth
> May threaten life and light,
> Remember God still rules the earth,
> And ravens fly at night.[13]

Our Lord continues to deliver good gifts and good news, and he will "meet all your needs according to the riches of his glory in Christ Jesus."

EPILOGUE

The Dawn Chorus

Rejoice in the Lord always. I will say it again: Rejoice!

—PHILIPPIANS 4:4

While other worldviews lead us to sit in the midst of life's joys, foreseeing the coming sorrows, Christianity empowers its people to sit in the midst of this world's sorrows, tasting the coming joy.

—TIM KELLER[1]

Listen.

You might hear it in the spring, before dawn, if you're camping (or at least willing to keep your bedroom window open). The earliest birdsong, perhaps the ethereal flute of a Wood Thrush, offers the opening notes. Its song is soon joined by another, and another—robin *churry-churrups* and cardinal *birdee-birdees* and the soft two-note greetings of chickadees. Doves coo, a nuthatch squeaks, a mockingbird freestyles. Finches and sparrows add longer phrases, along with a Downy Woodpecker's descending whinny and a Northern Parula's ascending buzz, and a tiny wren's singsong chatter somehow soars over it all.

I'm describing a forest-edged yard in the Carolinas, but it's the same concerto in other places, just with different instrumentation. I've heard it in India with a *really* obnoxious Asian Koel at three in the morning, joined at a more reasonable hour by drongos and bulbuls and chattering mynas. I've heard it in Costa Rica with early-rising kiskadees and trogons and pygmy owls and trees full of gregarious parakeets. Regardless of where you are on our planet, you're apt to experience it: a phenomenon known simply as the dawn chorus. It's twenty-five songs at once. But at the same time, it's *one* song, a whole that's far greater than the sum of its parts. The dawn chorus is the song under the songs—the one composite melody that gives meaning to all the others.

If the book of Philippians could be distilled into one word—the theme beneath the themes—it's simply the word *joy.*

Joy might not be the main thrust in any specific paragraphs of Paul's epistle, but it's a powerful undercurrent to the whole letter—so much so that it deserves its own headline, here at the end of this book. By my count, there are sixteen references to joy and rejoicing in just four chapters: a concentrated dose of jubilation. Joy is the blood in Paul's veins and the ink in his pen. We don't have to guess how Paul was feeling when he wrote this letter, because his heart overflows onto the parchment.

When he's not talking about his own joy-defined life, prayers, and situation (1:4, 18 twice; 2:2, 17 twice; 4:1, 10), he's cheering the Philippians on to embrace the same attitude (1:25; 2:18 twice, 28, 29; 3:1; 4:4 twice). He writes it as a command: *Be* joyous.

I know, none of us want to be told how to feel, especially in the midst of difficulty. Catchy jingles like "Don't worry, be happy" or "Hakuna matata" or Bob Marley's "Every little thing gonna be alright" (despite being spoken by three little birds) have never actually helped me in a crisis. Joy is something altogether different, and Paul exhorts his readers to take a deep breath of it. "Further, my brothers and sisters, rejoice in the Lord! It is no trouble for me to write the same things to you again, and it is a safeguard for you" (Philippians 3:1). *I don't mind repeating myself on this one, friends.* And then he does—again. "Rejoice in the Lord always. I will say it again: Rejoice!" (4:4).

The Christian life is joy. Paul's words to the Philippians ring hollow without it, as does the gospel itself. But what motivates this "song beneath the song"? It has to be more than circumstantial. We know that life's difficulties, like those Paul experienced in the Roman prison where he penned these words, can't steal joy. (As Wendell Berry wrote, "Be joyful though you have considered all the facts.")[2] And it's more than some sort of forced optimism or warm, fuzzy emotion we have to muster up.

Instead, for the Christian, joy is the triumph of faith—our gratitude for God's goodness looking *backward,* and our certainty of God's promises looking *forward.* It's not a fleeting emotion; it's the bedrock security that the Father is *for* us, the Son is *with* us, and the Spirit is *in* us. If these things are forefront, even if everything else in our life tanks, we can still have abounding joy. It can happen, Paul says, even when we're being painfully laid on the altar: "Even if I am being poured out like a drink offering on the sacrifice and service coming from your faith, I am glad and rejoice with all of you. So you too should be glad and rejoice with me" (Philippians 2:17–18).

Like I said, joy is faith-claimed victory, motivated by what's behind and what's ahead. You need an eye on each of those lenses, like a good set of binoculars. Try this: Consider a current hardship you might be facing—a situation where joy might be in short supply—and let's practice getting these two lenses focused.

Backward-motivated joy works like this: First, we might bring to mind some of the grander moments of God's provision in our lives—needs met, prayers answered, forgiveness granted. But for the biggest event, we dial further back, two thousand years or so, and savor the truth that we who deserve to perish in the wilting remnants of a fallen garden have instead been declared heirs of a blooming new creation. The Cross has removed the sting of guilt, and the perfect righteousness of Jesus has been credited to our account. These reminders focus our first lens with a rich depth of field.

But now for the second lens. *Forward*-motivated joy looks like this: He will still answer prayer. He will keep his promises. "No matter how many promises God has made, they are 'Yes' in Christ" (2 Corinthians 1:20). All God's promises to his people—commitments to albatross faithfulness and raven provision and sparrow safekeeping and every other bird picture we've discussed—will one day crescendo around a throne:

> Therefore God exalted him to the highest place
>   and gave him the name that is above every name,
> that at the name of Jesus every knee should bow,
>   in heaven and on earth and under the earth,
> and every tongue acknowledge that Jesus Christ is Lord,
>   to the glory of God the Father. (Philippians 2:9–11)

Our Savior will be inarguably recognized for who he is, either as an act of joyous worship or an act of final resignation. Knees will hit the dirt. Voices will proclaim his kingdom come. In the garden, creation unraveled under the cursed shadow of a tree. But in this Christ-exalted moment, our groaning world will beautifully come alive under a different tree:

> Then the angel showed me the river of the water of life, as clear as crystal, flowing from the throne of God and of the Lamb down the middle of the great street of the city. On each side of the river stood the tree of life, bearing twelve crops of fruit, yielding its fruit every month. And the leaves of the tree are for the healing of the nations. (Revelation 22:1–2)

The image is a new-and-improved, restored Eden—a garden fit for the goodness of eternity, set within a cityscape of perfect healing. This tree in the middle of the Holy City is the consummate picture of abundance, pouring out 24/7/365 fruit and gifting the world with nation-healing shade. Immersed in this unfathomable joy, how will we respond?

We will sing.

Song for a New Dawn

Why does a bird sing? From a purely biological view, birds sing to assert territory. They sing to attract a mate. They sing to stay in contact through their migration. They sing to teach or reassure their chicks. They sing to maintain the social bonds within their species. Any talk of singing for emotional expression is quickly debunked by the serious scientist as a frivolous waste of evolutionary energy. And yet, have you ever watched a bird singing because it seemingly *enjoyed* doing so? Scientists may steal our anthropomorphic fun, but poets know better—like Longfellow, who wrote, "How jubilant the happy birds renew / Their old, melodious madrigals of love!"[3]

In those final scenes of Revelation—which aren't final at all but simply the prologue to our forever and ever—the motivation for the music is pure, joyous worship,

> And they sang a new song, saying:
>
> "You are worthy to take the scroll
>   and to open its seals,
> because you were slain,
>   and with your blood you purchased for God
>   persons from every tribe and language and people
>   and nation." (Revelation 5:9)

Heaven's assembly, maybe with knees still bowed, will recite the "good good very good" of the Savior at the center of it all. The musical refrain is all about Jesus's absolute worthiness. But then that choir of purchased persons will rise to their incorruptible feet in joyous acclaim:

> After this I looked, and there before me was a great multitude that no one could count, from every nation, tribe, people and language, standing before the throne and before the Lamb. They were wearing white robes and were holding palm branches in their hands. And they cried out in a loud voice,
>
> "Salvation belongs to our God,
> who sits on the throne,
> and to the Lamb." (Revelation 7:9–10)

This is the dawn chorus. Do you hear it?

When I start getting too tactical in my kingdom-come imagination, I ponder how messy this scene will be for God to execute, respectfully speaking. I can't get my church to agree on four songs for Sunday morning; how in heaven (literally) will the song of the redeemed play out, when every language, culture, and historical era is represented? How will Gregorian chant meld with Nigerian drums and baroque harpsichord and a Nashville Stratocaster guitar? Are we using a pentatonic scale or an Indian raga? Will we count 4/4 time, or will we incorporate African polyrhythms? How will the expansive languages of Italian or Telugu match lines and verses with the more staccato feel of Icelandic or Japanese? Will we agree on what "in tune" means? I mean, are we using the pitch criteria of a concert cellist, an Indonesian gamelan player, or a Tuvan throat singer? How will we incorporate Bantu clicks and Old Norse inflections and ancient tongues long forgotten? How do we picture this auditory chaos, this outlandish sacred dissonance?

Easy. God gives us a preview of it every morning. As the dawn approaches, each bird lends its own earthy song, call, coo, hoot, whinny, whistle, buzz—all seemingly discordant and yet a miraculously melodic whole, stitching together into the song underneath all the songs. Emily Dickinson called it "A Music numerous as space— / But neighboring as Noon."[4] Sure, you can pick out the individual sounds if you know your birdsong, but close your eyes and you will feel yourself immersed in a melded whole, each instrument combined to form a unified early-morning symphony.

For the believer, our dawn chorus will be the full experience of the rhythm of the saints. It will be visceral and triumphant and wildly intense, resounding with praise from every tribe and nation and tongue. It will not be neat and tidy, flattened to the sensibilities of the key of C. But it will be *glorious.* A cacophony of devotion.

As I get older, I find myself looking forward to these scenes a lot more than I used to, awaiting the day of abundant trees and healed nations and the many-layered choir of the redeemed. I think this growing longing comes from the ever-deepening conviction that there's no other hope to fix this broken mess of a world, or the broken mess of me. I yearn for the day when, to quote a favorite saint from the choir, "the Lord takes by its corners this old world and shakes us forward and shakes us free."[5]

And so, until that symphony in which every culture contributes a chord, consider the birds—listening for the song under the song—and rejoice!

It is no trouble to write it again.

Rejoice!

ACKNOWLEDGMENTS

Some birds—like a Solitary Sandpiper, for instance—live an isolated hermit life. It's baked into the name, I guess; a Solitary Sandpiper even *migrates* alone. That's sort of what it feels like to start writing a book; you're working solo, you're keeping things largely secret to temper your own (and others') expectations, and you're probably the only one who truly cares if your project lives or dies. But you keep pecking away at it (bird pun).

Then somewhere along the way, one bird becomes two, two becomes four, and in time you've got yourself a small flock. That's what it feels like when your book gets a champion or two, like a friend who tells you to keep writing or a literary agent who sees potential or a publisher who decides to take a chance on you.

I'm so humbled and grateful to the Lord for the flock he's assembled to make this book happen. Thanks especially to two friends who flew in early in the process, as faithful advocates of the ornitheology blog idea. Matt Crossman is a gifted writer who gave me the advice to start small and see if anyone would read who wasn't either under duress or related to me by blood. And another author and friend, Mike Beates, encouraged me after every post, eventually forwarding one to a beloved colleague who also loves birds: Joni Eareckson Tada.

Thanks to Joni for exuding the undeniable spiritual gift of uplifting encouragement, for cheering on an untested rookie writer, offering to write the foreword, and graciously introducing me to her literary agent Andrew Wolgemuth.

Thanks to Andrew for guiding me patiently through all the questions of a first-time author and for introducing me to the talented team at WaterBrook & Multnomah, especially my editor and writing guru, Will Parker Anderson, the tip of the spear for this project. (It should be noted that, as an imprint of Penguin Random House, it was heartwarming to me to partner with a publisher that has a bird in their name.)

Thanks especially to Will for the unbelievably thorough edits and insights that have made this a better book—and also for connecting this project with Aedan Peterson, whose illustrations have wonderfully bridged the birds and the spiritual imagery of each chapter into artistic wholes. Aedan, you are a gifted pioneer of ornitheological art.

That's how a lone bird becomes a flock. But there's one more connection to celebrate; thanks to WaterBrook & Multnomah for helping to introduce me to you, the reader. It's an honor to have a few hours of your time to read this. Welcome to the ever-growing flock of ornitheologists; it's been my prayer that you would know Jesus better through these chapters and rest more joyously in his completed work for you.

Meanwhile, "other birds I have that are not of this flock" (John 10:16, paraphrased and taken painfully out of context), and I'm grateful for three of them in particular. First is the truly beautiful congregation of StoneBridge Church Community in Charlotte, North Carolina, which I have had the great privilege of pastoring for almost two decades and counting. Church, you have endured many a bird in sermon illustrations and cringeworthy puns and humored me with your own stories of backyard feeders, nests, and close encounters of the bird kind. More than that, you have persevered in our gospel community as we have sought to serve our neighbors, our city, and the ends of the earth. As we all continue to pursue Jesus and grow in grace, I'm so very grateful that we're family, placed together for God's kingdom purposes.

Second, I'm mindful of my ever-encouraging parents who have always supported my creative efforts, even through the seasons in which those efforts were undeniably weird. Thanks, Mom and Dad, for your steadfast presence through it all.

But most importantly, thank you to my wife, Beverly, and our "three little birds," Benjamin, Katelyn, and Timothy. All four of you bring something beautiful and unique to my life and to the world around you. To quote the great theologian and Dr. Seuss-ian P. D. Eastman, "I love my house, I love my nest. In all the world my nest is best." Or to quote the better theologian King David, "The boundary lines have fallen for me in pleasant places" (Psalm 16:6).

NOTES

Epigraph

1. Venerable Bede, "The Life and Miracles of St. Cuthbert, Bishop of Lindisfarne," in *The Ecclesiastical History of the English Nation,* trans. J. A. Giles (London, 1843), 41.

Foreword

1. Kevin Burrell, "Ornitheology: The Origins of a Splendid Made-Up Word," Ornitheology, July 4, 2020, www.ornitheology.com/post/ornitheology_explained.

Prayer of Preparation

1. Douglas McKelvey, ed., *Every Moment Holy,* vol. 3, *The Work of the People* (Rabbit Room Press, 2023), 153–54.

Prologue: Why Wise People Birdwatch

1. James Bryan Smith, *Rich Mullins: An Arrow Pointing to Heaven* (Broadman & Holman, 2000), 95.
2. Dale Ralph Davis, *1 Kings: The Wisdom and the Folly* (Christian Focus Publications, 2002), 49.

A Brief Note About Bird References

1. Kenn Kaufman, *The Birds That Audubon Missed: Discovery and Desire in the American Wilderness* (Avid Reader Press, 2024), ix.

Chapter 1: The Caged Bird Sings

1. Victor Hugo, *Les Misérables,* trans. Charles E. Wilbour, Modern Library Edition (Random House, 1992), 591.
2. In 2024, the Mealy Parrot (and other parrots of the genus *Amazona*)

was renamed the Mealy Amazon. Like I said, bird people love renaming birds.

3. A compelling case can also be made for an Ephesus jail either before or after the events of Acts 28, but I favor the traditional view that Philippians was written from Rome somewhere around A.D. 61.
4. William Blake, "The Schoolboy," in *Songs of Innocence and Experience: Showing the Two Contrary States of the Human Soul,* ed. George H. Cowling, Methuen's English Classics (Methuen, 1925), 38.

Chapter 2: Albatross Commitment

1. Charles Spurgeon, *The Complete Works of C. H. Spurgeon,* vol. 61, *Sermons 3440–3492* (Delmarva Publications, 2013).
2. Jess Thomson, "World's Oldest Known Bird Has Lost Her Mate of 60 Years," *Newsweek,* December 14, 2022, www.newsweek.com/oldest-boird-world-missing-mate-albatross-1767147.
3. Robert Greenall, "World's Oldest Known Wild Bird Lays Egg at 74," BBC, December 4, 2024, www.bbc.com/news/articles/c86w9n4jlvwo.
4. For a further explanation of a *karat berit* treaty, see O. Palmer Robertson, *The Christ of the Covenants* (Presbyterian and Reformed Publishing, 1980), 128–31.
5. Augustus Toplady, "A Debtor to Mercy Alone," Hymnary.org, https://hymnary.org/text/a_debtor_to_mercy_alone.

Chapter 3: The Empty Nest

1. C. S. Lewis, *Mere Christianity* (Macmillan, 1952; repr., Barbour, 1985), 168.
2. David Attenborough, *The Life of Birds* (Princeton University Press, 1998), 257.
3. Might I suggest "Ducklings Jump from Nest 50 Feet in the Air," Nature on PBS, YouTube video, April 7, 2015, www.youtube.com/watch?v=bDJw43BJtCE.
4. Paul R. Ehrlich, David S. Dobkin, and Darryl Wheye, "Precocial and Altricial Young," Stanford University, 1988, https://web.stanford.edu/group/stanfordbirds/text/essays/Precocial_and_Altricial.html.
5. Jennifer Ackerman, *The Genius of Birds* (Penguin Books, 2016), 57.
6. "Religion: Soul Saving," *Time,* January 23, 1978, time.com/archive/6853289/religion-soul-saving.
7. In adopting this strategy, we borrowed from the "Life-on-Life Missional Discipleship" model of Perimeter Church in Atlanta, Georgia. See lifeonlife.org.

Chapter 4: Bird Funerals

1. James K. A. Smith, *How to Inhabit Time: Understanding the Past, Facing the Future, Living Faithfully Now* (Brazos Press, 2022), 12–13.
2. As told in Jennifer Ackerman, *The Genius of Birds* (Penguin Books, 2016), 156.
3. W. R. Miller and R. M. Brigham, "'Ceremonial' Gathering of Black-Billed Magpies (*Pica pica*) After the Sudden Death of a Conspecific," *The Murrelet* 69, no. 3 (1998): 78–79, www.jstor.org/stable/3534036.
4. T. L. Iglesias, R. McElreath, and G. L. Patricelli, "Western Scrub-Jay Funerals: Cacophonous Aggregations in Response to Dead Conspecifics," *Animal Behaviour* 84, no. 5 (2012): 1103–11, https://doi.org/10.1016/j.anbehav.2012.08.007.
5. Ackerman, *Genius of Birds,* 155.
6. C. S. Lewis, *The Lion, the Witch, and the Wardrobe* (Geoffrey Bles, 1950; repr., HarperTrophy, 2005), 179.
7. J.R.R. Tolkien, *The Return of the King* (George Allen and Unwin, 1955; repr., Grafton, 1991), 277.
8. Richard Baxter, *The Saint's Everlasting Rest,* updated and abridged ed., ed. Tim Cooper (Crossway, 2022), 30–31.
9. Daniel Tompsett, "The Phoenix and the Early Church," *Vision,* 2011, https://foundations.vision.org/mythical-phoenix-in-early-church-writings-225.
10. Courtney Ellis, *Looking Up: A Birder's Guide to Hope Through Grief* (InterVarsity Press, 2024), 18.
11. Debbie Blue, *Consider the Birds: A Provocative Guide to the Birds of the Bible* (Abingdon Press, 2013), 77.
12. John Keats, "Ode to a Nightingale," Poetry Foundation, www.poetryfoundation.org/poems/44479/ode-to-a-nightingale.

Chapter 5: Birdnados & Murmurations

1. John Fawcett, "Blest Be the Tie That Binds," Hymnary.org, https://hymnary.org/text/blest_be_the_tie_that_binds.
2. Annie Dillard, *Pilgrim at Tinker Creek* (Harper Perennial, 1974), 42.
3. John Updike, "The Great Scarf of Birds," *The New Yorker,* October 27, 1962, 52.
4. Richard Wilbur, "An Event," in *Collected Poems: 1943–2004* (Harcourt, 2004), 347.
5. C. S. Lewis, *The Screwtape Letters* (Centenary, 1942; repr., Unwin Brothers, 1946), 16.
6. Joni Eareckson Tada and Steve Estes, *A Step Further: Growing Closer to*

God Through Hurt and Hardship (Zondervan, 1978), 33, emphasis original.

Chapter 6: Treecreeper Humility

1. James Montgomery, *A Poet's Portfolio; or, Minor Poems: In Three Books* (London, 1835), 179.
2. Andrew Van Dam and Alyssa Fowers, "Which Birds Are the Biggest Jerks at the Feeder? A Massive Data Analysis Reveals the Answer," *The Washington Post,* November 28, 2021, www.washingtonpost.com/business/2021/11/28/bird-feeder-pecking-order.
3. W. M. Tyler, "Brown Creeper," 1942, in *Life Histories of North American Birds,* vol. 2, *Land Birds,* ed. Arthur Cleveland Bent (Harper, 1960), 172.
4. Tyler, "Brown Creeper."
5. C. S. Lewis, *Mere Christianity* (Macmillan, 1952; repr., Barbour, 1985), 102.
6. William P. Farley, *Gospel-Powered Humility* (P&R Publishing, 2011), 25.
7. Lewis, *Mere Christianity,* 108.
8. John Dickson, *Humilitas: A Lost Key to Life, Love, and Leadership* (Zondervan, 2011), 99.
9. Philip Yancey, *The Jesus I Never Knew* (Zondervan, 1995), 32.
10. C. S. Lewis, *Miracles: A Preliminary Study* (Macmillan, 1947), 135.
11. Isaac Watts, "When I Survey the Wondrous Cross," Hymnary.org, https://hymnary.org/text/when_i_survey_the_wondrous_cross_watts.

Chapter 7: Honeyguide Partnerships

1. Thomas Brooks, *The Works of Thomas Brooks,* vol. 4 (Edinburgh, 1867), 81.
2. Purbita Saha and Claire Spottiswoode, "Meet the Greater Honeyguide, the Bird That Understands Humans," Audubon, August 22, 2016, www.audubon.org/magazine/meet-greater-honeyguide-bird-understands-humans.
3. Melanie Haiken, "These Birds Help Humans Find Honey. But It's Rare—and Getting Rarer," *National Geographic,* January 17, 2024, www.nationalgeographic.com/animals/article/birds-african-honeyguides-hunting.
4. Haiken, "These Birds Help Humans."
5. Sinclair Ferguson, *The Pundit's Folly: Chronicles of an Empty Life* (Banner of Truth, 1995), 74.
6. Tim Keller, "The Centrality of the Gospel," Redeemer City to City, January 1, 2000, https://redeemercitytocity.com/articles-stories/the-centrality-of-the-gospel.

Chapter 8: A Bird Mascot for the Church

1. N. T. Wright, *Surprised by Hope: Rethinking Heaven, the Resurrection, and the Mission of the Church* (HarperOne, 2008), 112.
2. Peter Berger, *Facing Up to Modernity: Excursions in Society, Politics, and Religion* (Basic Books, 1977), 18.
3. Russell Moore, *Onward: Engaging the Culture Without Losing the Gospel* (B&H Publishing, 2015), 8.
4. Frank Bolles, *Chocorua's Tenants* (Boston, 1895), 33.
5. Jim Robbins, *The Wonder of Birds: What They Tell Us About Ourselves, the World, and a Better Future* (Random House, 2018), 21–22.
6. I'm uncertain as to the exact origin of this story, but it was related to me by a member of the Abenaki tribe in Vermont.

Chapter 9: The Contentions & Courtesies of Crows

1. Groucho Marx, as reported in Sidney Skolsky, "Hollywood," *Daily News*, November 18, 1936, p. 62, col. 1.
2. John Marzluff and Tony Angell, *Gifts of the Crow: How Perception, Emotion, and Thought Allow Smart Birds to Behave Like Humans* (Atria, 2013), xii.
3. REO Speedwagon, "Take It on the Run," written by Gary Richrath, produced by Kevin Beamish, Kevin Cronin, Alan Gratzer, and Gary Richrath, track 5 on *Hi Infidelity*, Epic Records, 1980.
4. Garry Hamilton, "Crows Can Distinguish Faces in a Crowd," National Wildlife Federation, November 7, 2012, www.nwf.org/Magazines/National-Wildlife/2013/DecJan/Animals/Crows-Recognizing-Faces.
5. Marzluff and Angell, *Gifts of the Crow*, 107–8.
6. Marzluff and Angell, *Gifts of the Crow*, 109–11.
7. Jennifer Ackerman, *The Genius of Birds* (Penguin Books, 2016), 121.
8. Katy Sewall, "The Girl Who Gets Gifts from Birds," BBC, February 25, 2015, www.bbc.com/news/magazine-31604026.
9. Mark Winter, *Look at the Birds of the Air: Lessons from Birds in the Bible* (pub. by author, 2018), 106.

Chapter 10: Bowerbird Treasures

1. Victor Hugo, *Les Misérables*, trans. Charles E. Wilbour, Modern Library Edition (Random House, 1992), 145.
2. William Shakespeare, *The Merchant of Venice*, ed. Barbara A. Mowat and Paul Werstine (Simon & Schuster, 2010), act 2, scene 7, line 73. (Though most of us today have changed the verb to *glitters*.)

3. Son of Laughter, "Grace Is Gold," written by Chris Slaten, produced by Ben Shive, track 2 on *The Mantis and the Moon,* released by Son of Laughter, 2013, https://son-of-laughter.com.
4. Martin Luther, quoted in Roland Bainton, *Here I Stand: A Life of Martin Luther* (Abingdon, 1950), 45.

Chapter 11: Tern Pursuits

1. John Stott, *The Birds Our Teachers: Essays in Orni-Theology,* collector's ed. (H. Shaw, 1999; repr., Candle Books, 2007), 51.
2. Erwin McManus, *Chasing Daylight: Seize the Power of Every Moment* (Thomas Nelson, 2002), back cover copy.
3. "Why do you wear a mask? Were you burned by acid, or something like that?" "Oh no, it's just that they're terribly comfortable. I think everyone will be wearing them in the future." *The Princess Bride,* written by William Goldman, directed by Rob Reiner (20th Century Fox, 1987).
4. Scott Weidensaul, *A World on the Wing: The Global Odyssey of Migratory Birds* (W. W. Norton, 2021), 11.
5. Dane Ortlund, *Deeper: Real Change for Real Sinners* (Crossway, 2021), 114–15.

Chapter 12: The Homing of Pigeons

1. Frederick Buechner, *Godric* (Atheneum, 1980), 37.
2. Stephen Moss, *Ten Birds That Changed the World* (Basic Books, 2023), 69.
3. Kathleen Rooney, *Cher Ami and Major Whittlesey* (Penguin, 2020), 1.
4. Jim Robbins, *The Wonder of Birds: What They Tell Us About Ourselves, the World, and a Better Future* (Random House, 2017), 238.
5. C. S. Lewis, *Mere Christianity* (Macmillan, 1952; repr., Barbour, 1985), 115.
6. Jennifer Ackerman, *The Genius of Birds* (Penguin Books, 2016), 272.
7. Lin-Manuel Miranda and Opetaia Foa'i, "We Know the Way," written by Lin-Manuel Miranda and Opetaia Foa'i, produced by Chris Montan, Lin-Manuel Miranda, Mark Mancina, and Opetaia Foa'i, track 5 on *Moana: Original Motion Picture Soundtrack,* Walt Disney, 2016.
8. Dennis Johnson, *Philippians,* Reformed Expository Commentary (P&R Publishing, 2013), 226.
9. Zack Eswine, *Sensing Jesus: Life and Ministry as a Human Being* (Crossway, 2013), 58.
10. Andrew Peterson, *The God of the Garden: Thoughts on Creation, Culture, and the Kingdom* (B&H Publishing, 2021), 168.
11. Rich Mullins, "Here in America," written by Rich Mullins, produced by

Reed Arvin, track 1 on *A Liturgy, a Legacy & a Ragamuffin Band,* Reunion Records, 1993.

12. Eswine, *Sensing Jesus,* 64.
13. Rick Rusaw and Brian Mavis, *The Neighboring Church: Getting Better at What Jesus Says Matters Most* (Thomas Nelson, 2016), 75.
14. Lewis, *Mere Christianity,* 113.

Chapter 13: Considering Sparrows

1. Martin Luther, *Luther's Works,* vol. 21, *The Sermon on the Mount and the Magnificat,* ed. Jaroslav Pelikan (Concordia, 1956), 197.
2. Helen Briggs, "More Than a Billion Sparrows in the World, Study Finds," BBC, May 17, 2021, www.bbc.com/news/science-environment -57150571.
3. John Stott, *The Birds Our Teachers: Essays in Orni-Theology,* collector's ed. (H. Shaw, 1999; repr., Candle Books, 2007), 35.
4. Walter Barrows, *The English Sparrow (Passer domesticus) in North America: Especially in Its Relation to Agriculture* (Washington, DC, 1889), 35.
5. Barrows, *The English Sparrow,* 35.
6. Gary Alan Fine and Lazaros Christoforides, "Dirty Birds, Filthy Immigrants, and the English Sparrow War: Metaphorical Linkage in Constructing Social Problems," *Symbolic Interaction* 14, no. 4 (Winter 1991): abstract.
7. Mabel Osgood Wright and Elliott Coues, *Citizen Bird: Scenes from Bird-Life in Plain English for Beginners* (New York, 1897), 182.
8. "Red China: Death to Sparrows," *Time,* May 5, 1958, https://time.com/archive/6800787/red-china-death-to-sparrows.
9. I'm grateful to Debbie Blue's recounting of some of this history in her book *Consider the Birds: A Provocative Guide to the Birds of the Bible* (Abingdon Press, 2013), 131–36.
10. Briggs, "More Than a Billion Sparrows."
11. David Allen Sibley, *What It's Like to Be a Bird: From Flying to Nesting, Eating to Singing—What Birds Are Doing, and Why* (Alfred A. Knopf, 2020), 160.
12. Civilla D. Martin, "His Eye Is on the Sparrow," Hymnary.org, https://hymnary.org/text/why_should_i_feel_discouraged_why_should.
13. Joni Eareckson Tada, *When Is It Right to Die? Suicide, Euthanasia, Suffering, Mercy* (Zondervan, 1992), 23–25, 178–79.

Chapter 14: Mockingbird Maturity

1. Andrew Bonar, *Memoir and Remains of the Rev. Robert Murray M'Cheyne* (Edinburgh, 1892), 282.

2. Harper Lee, *To Kill a Mockingbird* (Warner Books, 1960), 90.
3. For example, see Hannah Price, "Birds of a Feather Talk Together," *Australian Geographic,* September 15, 2011, www.australiangeographic.com.au/news/2011/09/birds-of-a-feather-talk-together/.
4. Tim Keller with Kathy Keller, *The Meaning of Marriage: Facing the Complexities of Commitment with the Wisdom of God* (Dutton, 2011), 73.
5. Tim Chester, "10 Things You Should Know About John Stott," Crossway.org, June 25, 2020, www.crossway.org/articles/10-things-you-should-know-about-john-stott.

Chapter 15: The Strength of Eagles

1. J.R.R. Tolkien, *The Hobbit, or There and Back Again* (Houghton Mifflin, 1937; repr., Mariner Books, 2013), 106.
2. Philippians 4:13. That's the English Standard Version. You might have learned it as "I can do all things through Christ which strengtheneth me" (King James Version), but the word "Christ" doesn't appear in the earliest Greek manuscripts, though clearly this is who Paul meant by the pronoun.
3. Noah Stryker, *Birding Without Borders: An Obsession, a Quest, and the Biggest Year in the World* (Mariner Books, 2017), 56.
4. "White-Tailed Eagle," eBird, https://ebird.org/species/whteag.
5. Pliny the Elder, quoted in Gene Stratton-Porter, *Birds of the Bible* (Createspace, 2016), 74.
6. Perhaps the only aspect of an eagle we've found uninspiring is its voice. It's an inconvenient truth, but when you see a Bald Eagle in a movie, commercial, or any other source that's not a nature documentary, the call you'll most likely hear is an overdub of a Red-tailed Hawk. Admittedly, they *do* sound cooler.
7. Jeremiah Burroughs, *The Rare Jewel of Christian Contentment* (1648; repr., Banner of Truth, 2002), 19.
8. Paige Benton Brown, "Singled Out by God for Good," Joni and Friends, November 29, 2019, www.joniandfriends.org/wp-content/uploads/2019/11/11-29-19-Singled-Out-By-God-For-Good.pdf, emphasis added.
9. Adrian Junius, quoted in Burroughs, *Rare Jewel of Christian Contentment,* 56.
10. U2, "I Still Haven't Found What I'm Looking For," produced by Daniel Lanois and Brian Eno, track 2 on *The Joshua Tree,* Island Records, 1987.
11. Luke Naylor and Andrew Raedeke, "Tracking the Mallard Migration," Ducks Unlimited, August 13, 2013, www.ducks.org/conservation/waterfowl-research-science/understanding-waterfowl-tracking-the-mallard-migration.

12. "Ken Blanchard Quotes," BrainyQuote, accessed September 12, 2025, www.brainyquote.com/quotes/ken_blanchard_173322.

Chapter 16: The Provision of Ravens

1. John Piper, "Elijah: Part 1," Desiring God, November 29, 1992, www.desiringgod.org/articles/elijah-part-1.
2. Debbie Blue, *Consider the Birds: A Provocative Guide to the Birds of the Bible* (Abingdon Press, 2013), 192–93.
3. Edgar Allan Poe, "The Raven," *The Complete Poems of Edgar Allan Poe* (Barnes & Noble, 1994), 69.
4. God says he won't just withhold the rain but even the *dew*—a devastating eco-catastrophe for a region that experienced such plentiful dew that (in the spring and fall) you could still grow a successful crop without rain. It's the same region where Gideon made sheepskin dew-dares with God in Judges 6. And now the Lord is sucking up every ounce of the nation's moisture. Harsh providence.
5. Jennifer Ackerman, *The Genius of Birds* (Penguin Books, 2016), 123.
6. Ackerman, *The Genius of Birds,* 152–53.
7. Edward A. Armstrong, *The Folklore of Birds: An Enquiry into the Origin and Distribution of Some Magico-Religious Traditions* (Houghton Mifflin, 1958), 71.
8. Stephen Moss, *Ten Birds That Changed the World* (Basic Books, 2023), 20.
9. "Tower of London: 'Adventurous' Ravens Have Their Wings Clipped," BBC, January 4, 2024, www.bbc.com/news/uk-england-london-67881521.
10. Tim Keller, *Preaching: Communicating Faith in an Age of Skepticism* (Viking, 2015), 231.
11. Blue, *Consider the Birds,* 201.
12. Elvina M. Hall, "Jesus Paid It All," Hymnary.org, https://hymnary.org/text/i_hear_the_savior_say_thy_strength_indee.
13. Piper, "Elijah: Part 1."

Epilogue: The Dawn Chorus

1. Tim Keller, *Walking with God Through Pain and Suffering* (Penguin Books, 2013), 31.
2. Wendell Berry, "Manifesto: The Mad Farmer Liberation Front," in *The Country of Marriage* (Harcourt Brace Jovanovich, 1973), 17.
3. Henry Wadsworth Longfellow, "The Poet's Tale; The Birds of Killingworth," Maine Historical Society, www.hwlongfellow.org/poems_poem.php?pid=2047.

4. Emily Dickinson, "The Birds Begun at Four O'clock," *The Complete Poems of Emily Dickinson,* ed. Thomas H. Johnson (Little, Brown and Company, 1960), 381.
5. Rich Mullins, "Calling Out Your Name," written by Rich Mullins, produced by Reed Arvin, track 6 on *The World as Best as I Remember It,* vol. 1, Reunion Records, 1991.

ABOUT THE AUTHOR

Kevin Burrell is the co-lead pastor of StoneBridge Church Community in Charlotte, North Carolina. An avid birder, he blends his pastoral heart and avian interests on his blog, Ornitheology, where he utilizes birds as illustrations of the Christian life and invites readers to look up—literally and spiritually—to notice the grace of God in ordinary moments.

Kevin is a native of Upstate New York. Prior to his current role, he served churches in Athens, Georgia, and Orlando, Florida. He lives in Charlotte with his wife Beverly, three children, and five bird feeders.